# vacation-style
# HOME PLANS

## Vacation-Style Home Plans

**Vacation-Style Home Plans** is a collection of our best-selling vacation-style homes in a variety of styles. These plans cover a wide range of architectural styles. A broad assortment is presented to match a wide variety of lifestyles and budgets. Each design page features floor plans, a front view of the house, interior square footage of the home, number of bedrooms, baths, garage size and foundation types. All floor plans show room and exterior dimensions.

## Technical Specifications

At the time the construction drawings were prepared, every effort was made to ensure that these plans and specifications meet nationally recognized building codes (BOCA, Southern Building Code Congress and others). Because national building codes change or vary from area to area some drawing modifications and/or the assistance of a professional designer or architect may be necessary to comply with your local codes or to accommodate specific building site conditions. We advise you to consult with your local building official for information regarding codes governing your area.

## Blueprint Ordering - Fast and Easy

Your ordering is made simple by following the instructions on page 7. See page 6 for more information on which types of blueprint packages are available and how many plan sets to order.

## Your Home, Your Way

The blueprints you receive are a master plan for building your new home. They start you on your way to what may well be the most rewarding experience of your life.

COVER HOME The house shown on the front cover is plan #M03-022D-0018 and is featured on page 168. Photo courtesy of HDA, Inc., St. Louis, Missouri.

VACATION-STYLE HOME PLANS is published by HDA, Inc., 944 Anglum Road, St. Louis, MO, 63042. All rights reserved. Reproduction in whole or in part without written permission of the publisher is prohibited. Printed in U.S.A. © 2007. Artist drawings and photos shown in this publication may vary slightly from the actual working drawings. Some photos are shown in mirror reverse. Please refer to the floor plan for accurate layout.

# CONTENTS

# MENARDS®

Current printing   5   4   3

## "Thanks to MENARDS®, finding and building our Dream Home has never been easier."

Thinking about building your dream home? Or, perhaps you are interested in a vacation home or downsizing to a single story home? Choosing a home plan can be a daunting task.

This book of Vacation-Style Home Plans has been designed to make the search simple and easy. Browse the pages of this book and look for the style that best suits your family and your needs. These plans have been chosen from top designers from across the country and can provide to you the perfect home that will truly be a place of refuge for your whole family for years to come.

This book is the perfect place to begin your search for the home of your dreams. You will find the expected beauty you want and the functional efficiency you need, all designed with unmatched quality.

Also, keep in mind, this book contains helpful articles for understanding what kind of plan package you may need as well as other helpful building aids to make the process even easier.

When you have made this decision visit your local MENARDS® store to place your order and partner with one of their friendly team members to walk you through the process.

MENARDS® is dedicated to assist you through the entire home decision process.

# What's The Right Plan For You?

Choosing a home plan is an exciting but difficult task. Many factors play a role in what home plan is best for you and your family. To help you get started, we have pinpointed some of the major factors to consider when searching for your dream home. Take the time to evaluate your family's needs and you will have an easier time sorting through all of the home plans offered in this book.

**Budget:** The first thing to consider is your budget. Many items take part in this budget, from ordering the blueprints to the last doorknob purchased. Once you have found your dream home plan, visit the **MENARDS®** Building Materials Desk to get a cost-to-build estimate to ensure that the finished product is still within your price range.

**Family Lifestyle:** After your budget is deciphered, you need to assess you and your family's lifestyle needs. Think about the stage of life you are at now, and what stages you will be going through in the future. Ask yourself questions to figure out how much room you need now and if you will need room for expansion. Are you married? Do you have children? How many children do you plan on having? Are you an empty-nester?

Incorporate in your planning any frequent guests you may have, including elderly parents, grandchildren or adult children who may live with you.

Does your family entertain a lot? If so, think about the rooms you will need to do so. Will you need both formal and informal spaces? Do you need a gourmet kitchen? Do you need a game room and/or a wet bar?

Experts in the field suggest that the best way to determine your needs is to begin by listing everything you like or dislike about your current home.

**Floor Plan Layouts:** When looking through our home plans, imagine yourself walking through the house. Consider the flow from the entry to the living, sleeping and gathering areas. Does the layout ensure privacy for the master bedroom? Does the garage enter near the kitchen for easy unloading? Does the placement of the windows provide enough privacy from any neighboring properties? Do you plan on using furniture you already have? Will this furniture fit in the appropriate rooms? When you find a plan you want to purchase, be sure to picture yourself actually living in it.

**Exterior Spaces:** There are many different home styles ranging from Traditional to Contemporary. Flip through and find which style most appeals to you and the neighborhood in which you plan to build. Also think of your site and how the entire house will fit on this site. Picture any landscaping you plan on incorporating into the design. Using your imagination is key when choosing a home plan.

Choosing a home plan can be an intimidating experience. Asking yourself these questions before you get started on the search will help you through the process. With our large selection of multiple styles we are certain you will find your dream home in the following pages.

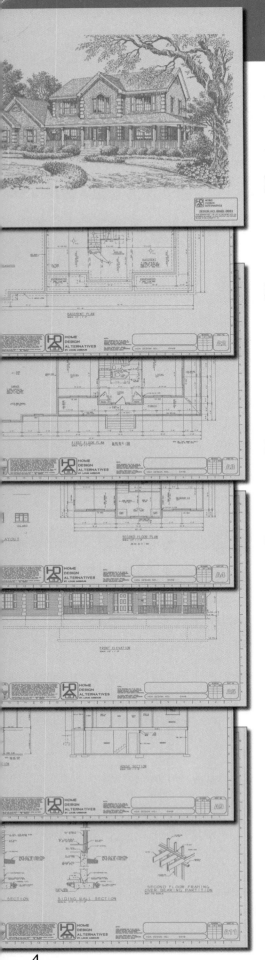

# Our Blueprint Packages Offer ...

Quality plans for building your future, with extras that provide unsurpassed value, ensure good construction and long-term enjoyment.

## 1. Cover Sheet

Included with many of the plans, the cover sheet is the artist's rendering of the exterior of the home. It will give you an idea of how your home will look when completed and landscaped.

## 2. Foundation

The foundation plan shows the layout of the basement, walk-out basement, crawl space, slab or pier foundation. All necessary notations and dimensions are included. See plan page for the foundation types included. If the home plan you choose does not have your desired foundation type, call or visit any **MENARDS** and they can advise you on how to customize your foundation to suit your specific needs or site conditions.

## 3. Floor Plans

The floor plans show the placement of walls, doors, closets, plumbing fixtures, electrical outlets, columns, and beams for each level of the home.

## 4. Interior Elevations

Interior elevations provide views of special interior elements such as fireplaces, kitchen cabinets, built-in units and other features of the home.

## 5. Exterior Elevations

Exterior elevations illustrate the front, rear and both sides of the house, with all details of exterior materials and the required dimensions.

## 6. Sections

Show detail views of the home or portions of the home as if it were sliced from the roof to the foundation. This sheet shows important areas such as load-bearing walls, stairs, joists, trusses and other structural elements, which are critical for proper construction.

## 7. Details

Show how to construct certain components of your home, such as the roof system, stairs, deck, etc.

# More Helpful Building Aids

Your Blueprint Package will contain the necessary construction information to build your home. We also offer the following products and services to save you time and money in the building process.

## Material List

Material lists are available for all the plans in this book. Each list gives you the quantity, dimensions and description of the building materials necessary to construct your home. You'll get faster and more accurate bids from your contractor while saving money by paying for only the materials you need. To receive a free home plan estimate call or visit any **MENARDS®** Building Materials Desk.

Discount Price: $125.00 - Menards SKU 100-3422
Note: Material lists are not refundable.

## Express Delivery

Most orders are processed within 24 hours of receipt. Please allow 7-10 business days for delivery. If you need to place a rush order, please call or visit any **MENARDS®** store to order by 11:00 a.m. Monday-Friday CST and specify you would like express service (allow 1-2 business days.

Discount Price: $40.00
Menards SKU 194-4356

## Technical Assistance

If you have additional questions, call our technical support line at 1-314-770-2228 between 8:00 a.m. and 5:00 p.m. Monday-Friday CST. Whether it involves design modifications or field assistance, our designers are extremely familiar with all of our designs and will be happy to help you. We want your home to be everything you expect it to be.

# Other Great Products . . .

## The Legal Kit

Avoid many legal pitfalls and build your home with confidence using the forms and contracts featured in this kit. Included are request for proposal documents, various fixed price and cost plus contracts, instructions on how and when to use each form, warranty statements and more. Save time and money before you break ground on your new home or start a remodeling project. All forms are reproducible. The kit is ideal for homebuilders and contractors.

Discount Price: $35.00 - Menards SKU 100-3422

## Detail Plan Packages - Electrical, Plumbing & Framing Packages

Three separate packages offer homebuilders details for constructing various foundations; numerous floor, wall and roof framing techniques; simple to complex residential wiring; sump pump and water softener hookups; plumbing connection methods; installation of septic systems, and more. Each package includes three dimensional illustrations and a glossary of terms. Purchase one or all three. Note: These drawings do not pertain to a specific home plan.

Discount Price: $20.00 each or all three for $40.00
Menards SKU 100-3422

# What Kind Of Plan Package Do You Need?

Now that you've found the home you've been looking for, here are some suggestions on how to make your Dream Home a reality. To get started, order the type of plans that fit your particular situation.

## Your Choices

### The One-Set Study Package*

We offer a One-set plan package so you can study your home in detail. This one set is considered a study set and is marked "not for construction." It is a copyright violation to reproduce blueprints.

### The Minimum 5-Set Package*

If you're ready to start the construction process, this 5-Set package is the minimum number of blueprint sets you will need. It will require keeping close track of each set so they can be used by multiple subcontractors and tradespeople.

### The Standard 8-Set Package*

For best results in terms of cost, schedule and quality of construction, we recommend you order eight (or more) sets of blueprints. Besides one set for yourself, additional sets of blueprints will be required by your mortgage lender, local building department, general contractor and all subcontractors working on foundation, electrical, plumbing, heating/air conditioning, carpentry work, etc.

### Reproducible Masters

If you wish to make some minor design changes, you'll want to order reproducible masters. These drawings contain the same information as the blueprints but are printed on reproducible paper that is easy to alter and clearly indicates your right to copy or reproduce. This will allow your builder or a local design professional to make the necessary drawing changes without the major expense of redrawing the plans. This package also allows you to print copies of the modified plans as needed. The right of building only one structure from these plans is licensed exclusively to the buyer. You may not use this design to build a second or multiple dwelling(s) without purchasing another blueprint. Each violation of the Copyright Law is punishable in a fine.

### Mirror Reverse Sets

Plans can be printed in mirror reverse. These plans are useful when the house would fit your site better if all the rooms were on the opposite side than shown. They are simply a mirror image of the original drawings causing the lettering and dimensions to read backwards. Therefore, when ordering mirror reverse drawings, you must purchase at least one set of right-reading plans.

* Additional sets of the same plan ordered are available only within 90 days after purchase of original plan package.

Discount Price: $45.00 - Menards SKU 194-4330

6

# How To Order Home Plans

## You've found your Dream Home, now what?

### Follow these simple steps

1. Review the article on page 6 to decide what type of plan package you need.
2. To order, call or visit any **MENARDS** store and go to the Building Materials Desk.

To locate the **MENARDS** store nearest you go to **www.Menards.com**, click on Store Service then click on the Store locator.

*Artist drawings and photos shown in this publication may vary slightly from the actual working drawings. Some photos are shown in mirror reverse. Please refer to the floor plan for accurate layout.*

## BLUEPRINT SKU PRICING

| PRICE CODE | | 1-SET STUDY | 5-SET PLAN | 8-SET PLAN | REPRO. MASTERS |
|---|---|---|---|---|---|
| AAA | Menards SKU | 194-3920 | 194-3933 | 194-3946 | 194-3959 |
| | Discount Price | $310 | $380 | $425 | $525 |
| AA | Menards SKU | 194-3962 | 194-3975 | 194-3988 | 194-3991 |
| | Discount Price | $410 | $480 | $525 | $625 |
| A | Menards SKU | 194-4000 | 194-4084 | 194-4165 | 194-4246 |
| | Discount Price | $470 | $540 | $585 | $685 |
| B | Menards SKU | 194-4013 | 194-4097 | 194-4178 | 194-4259 |
| | Discount Price | $530 | $600 | $645 | $745 |
| C | Menards SKU | 194-4026 | 194-4107 | 194-4181 | 194-4262 |
| | Discount Price | $585 | $655 | $700 | $800 |
| D | Menards SKU | 194-4039 | 194-4110 | 194-4194 | 194-4275 |
| | Discount Price | $635 | $705 | $750 | $850 |
| E | Menards SKU | 194-4042 | 194-4123 | 194-4204 | 194-4288 |
| | Discount Price | $695 | $765 | $810 | $910 |
| F | Menards SKU | 194-4055 | 194-4136 | 194-4217 | 194-4291 |
| | Discount Price | $750 | $820 | $865 | $965 |
| G | Menards SKU | 194-4068 | 194-4149 | 194-4220 | 194-4301 |
| | Discount Price | $850 | $920 | $965 | $1065 |
| H | Menards SKU | 194-4071 | 194-4152 | 194-4233 | 194-4314 |
| | Discount Price | $945 | $1015 | $1060 | $1160 |

*Many of our plans are available in CAD. For availability, call or visit any* **MENARDS** *store and go to the Building Materials Desk.*

## OTHER PRODUCTS & BUILDING AIDS

### MIRROR REVERSE*
| Menards SKU | 194-4327 |
|---|---|
| Discount Price | $15 |

### ADDITIONAL SETS**
| Menards SKU | 194-4330 |
|---|---|
| Discount Price | $45 |

### MATERIAL LIST**
| Menards SKU | 100-3422 |
|---|---|
| Discount Price | $125 |

### EXPRESS DELIVERY
| Menards SKU | 194-4356 |
|---|---|
| Discount Price | $40 |

### LEGAL KIT
| Menards SKU | 100-3422 |
|---|---|
| Discount Price | $35 |

### DETAIL PLAN PACKAGES
ELECTRICAL, PLUMBING & FRAMING - ALL SAME SKU
| Menards SKU | 100-3422 |
|---|---|
| Discount Price | $20 EA. |
| | 3 FOR $40 |

\* See page 6
\*\* Available only within 90 days after puchase of plan package of same plan

If at any time you feel you may need assistance in the field while building, HDA offers a technical assistance line for answering building questions pertaining to your specific plan. Please call 314-770-2228 Monday-Friday between 8:00am and 5:00pm CST and our professional design staff will be happy to help.

Please note: All blueprints are printed in response to your order, so we cannot honor requests for refunds. However, if for some reason you find that the plan you have purchased does not meet your requirements, you may exchange that plan for another plan in our collection within 90 days of purchase. At the time of the exchange, you will be charged a processing fee of 25% of your original plan package price, plus the difference in price between the plan packages (if applicable) and the cost to ship the new plans to you. Keep in mind, reproducible drawings can only be exchanged if the package is unopened and material lists can only be purchased within 90 days of purchasing the plan package.

# Making Changes To Your Plan

We understand that it is difficult to find blueprints for a home that will meet all your needs. That is why HDA, Inc. (Home Design Alternatives) is pleased to offer home plan modification services.

**Typical home plan modifications include:**
- Changing foundation type
- Adding square footage to a plan
- Changing exterior wall framing from 2x4 to 2x6
- Changing wall heights
- Changing the entry into a garage
- Changing a two-car garage to a three-car garage or making a garage larger
- Redesigning kitchen, baths, and bedrooms
- Changing exterior elevations
- Or most other home plan modifications you may desire!

**Some home plan modifications we cannot make include:**
- Mirror-reversing the plans
- Adapting/engineering plans to meet local building codes
- Combining parts of two different plans (due to copyright laws)

**Our plan modification service is easy to use. Simply:**

1. Decide on the modifications you want. For the most accurate quote, be as detailed as possible and refer to rooms in the same manner as the floor plan (i.e. if the floor plan refers to a "den," use "den" in your description). Including a sketch of the modified floor plan is always helpful.

2. Visit any **MENARDS®** Building Materials Desk and request an HDA Custom Change Form.

3. Within two business days, you or your Menards store will receive your quote - that's up to you. Quotes do not include the cost of the reproducible masters required for our designer to legally make changes. For example, if your quote is $850 and the reproducible masters for your plan are $800, your order total will be $1650 including shipping and handling charges.

4. Call the number on the quote to accept and purchase the reproducible masters from the **MENARDS®** Building Materials Desk.

5. Our designer will send you up to three drafts to verify your initial changes. Extra costs apply after the third draft. If additional changes are made that alter the original request, extra charges may be incurred.

6. Once you approve a draft with the final changes, we then make the changes to the reproducible masters by adding additional sheets. The original reproducible masters (with no changes) plus your new changed sheets will be shipped to you.

**Other Important Information:**

• Plans cannot be redrawn in reverse format. All modifications will be made to match the reproducible master's original layout. Once you receive the plans, you can make reverse copies at your local copy shop.

• Our staff designer will provide the first draft for your review within 4 weeks (plus shipping time) of receiving your order.

• You will receive up to three drafts to review before your original changes are modified. The first draft will totally encompass all modifications based on your original request. Additional changes not included in your original request will be charged separately at an hourly rate of $75 or a flat quoted rate.

• Modifications will be drawn on a separate sheet with the changes shown and a note to see the main sheet for details. For example, a floor plan sheet from the original set (i.e. Sheet 3) would be followed by a new floor plan sheet with changes (i.e. Sheet A-3).

• Plans are drawn to meet national building codes. Modifications will not be drawn to any particular state or county codes, thus we cannot guarantee that the revisions will meet your local building codes. You may be required to have a local architect or designer review the plans in order to have them comply with your state or county building codes.

• Time and cost estimates are good for 90 calendar days.

• All modification requests need to be submitted in writing. Verbal requests will not be accepted.

## Easy Steps for FAST service

Visit any **MENARDS®** Building Materials Desk and request an HDA Custom Change Form.
Simply follow the instructions to receive your quote within two business days.

# Plan #M03-017D-0010

*Iris*

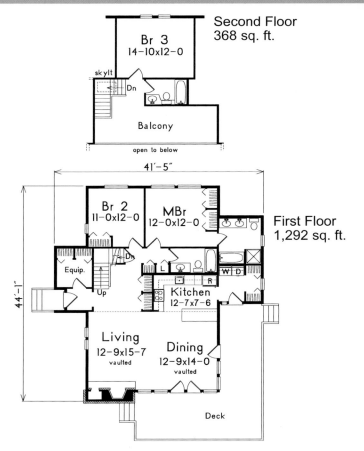

Second Floor
368 sq. ft.

Br 3
14-10x12-0

skylt

Dn

Balcony

open to below

41'-5"

44'-1"

Br 2
11-0x12-0

MBr
12-0x12-0

First Floor
1,292 sq. ft.

Equip.

Up

Kitchen
12-7x7-6

Living
12-9x15-7
vaulted

Dining
12-9x14-0
vaulted

Deck

## Dramatic Expanse Of Windows

1,660 total square feet of living area

### Special features

- Energy efficient home with 2" x 6" exterior walls
- Convenient gear and equipment room
- Spacious living and dining rooms look even larger with the openness of the foyer and kitchen
- Large wrap-around deck is a great plus for outdoor living
- Broad balcony overlooks living and dining rooms
- 3 bedrooms, 3 baths
- Partial basement/crawl space foundation, drawings also include slab foundation

### Price Code C

**To order this plan, visit the Menards Building Materials Desk.**

*Mayland*

## Country-Style Home With Large Front Porch

1,501 total square feet of living area

### Special features

- Spacious kitchen with dining area is open to the outdoors
- Convenient utility room is adjacent to the garage
- Master bedroom features a private bath, dressing area and access to the large covered porch
- Large family room creates openness
- 3 bedrooms, 2 baths, 2-car side entry garage
- Basement foundation, drawings also include crawl space and slab foundations

### Price Code B

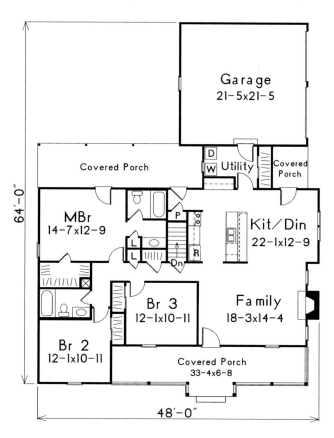

10

**To order this plan, visit the Menards Building Materials Desk.**

*Provider II*

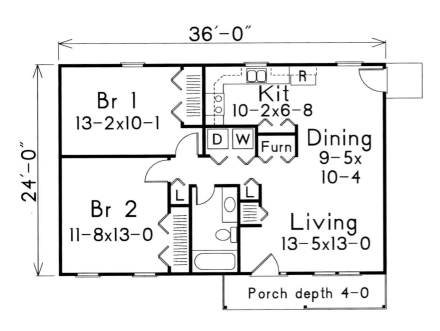

## Perfect Home For A Small Family

864 total square feet of living area

### Special features

- L-shaped kitchen with convenient pantry is adjacent to the dining area
- Easy access to laundry area, linen closet and storage closet
- Both bedrooms include ample closet space
- 2 bedrooms, 1 bath
- Crawl space foundation, drawings also include basement and slab foundations

### Price Code AAA

**To order this plan, visit the Menards Building Materials Desk.**

*Dunwood*

## Compact Home For Functional Living

1,220 total square feet of living area

### Special features

- A vaulted ceiling adds luxury to the living room and master bedroom
- Spacious living room is accented with a large fireplace and hearth
- Gracious dining area is adjacent to the convenient wrap-around kitchen
- Washer and dryer are handy to the bedrooms
- Covered porch entry adds appeal
- Rear deck adjoins dining area
- 3 bedrooms, 2 baths, 2-car drive under garage
- Basement foundation

### Price Code A

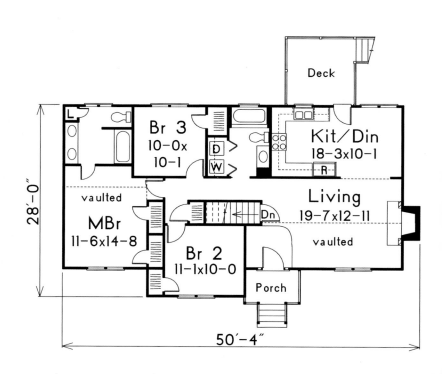

Deck

Br 3
10-0x
10-1

Kit/Din
18-3x10-1

vaulted

MBr
11-6x14-8

Living
19-7x12-11

Dn

vaulted

Br 2
11-1x10-0

Porch

28'-0"

50'-4"

To order this plan, visit the Menards Building Materials Desk.

*Woodsmill*

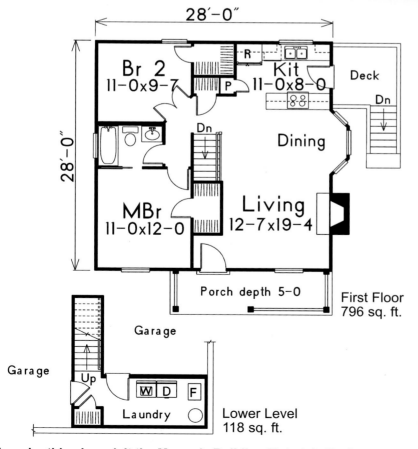

28'-0"

Br 2
11-0x9-7

Kit
11-0x8-0

Deck

R

P

Dn

Dn

Dining

28'-0"

MBr
11-0x12-0

Living
12-7x19-4

Porch depth 5-0

**First Floor
796 sq. ft.**

Garage

Garage

Up

W D F

Laundry

**Lower Level
118 sq. ft.**

## Small Home Is Remarkably Spacious

914 total square feet of living area

### Special features

- Large porch for leisure evenings
- Dining area with bay window, open stair and pass-through kitchen create openness
- Basement includes generous garage space, storage area, finished laundry and mechanical room
- 2 bedrooms, 1 bath, 2-car drive under garage
- Basement foundation

### Price Code AA

**To order this plan, visit the Menards Building Materials Desk.**

13

## Cedarwood

## Rambling Country Bungalow

1,475 total square feet of living area

### Special features

■ Family room features a high ceiling and prominent corner fireplace

■ Kitchen with island counter and garden window makes a convenient connection between the family and dining rooms

■ Hallway leads to three bedrooms all with large walk-in closets

■ Covered breezeway joins the main house and garage

■ Full-width covered porch entry lends a country touch

■ 3 bedrooms, 2 baths, 2-car detached side entry garage

■ Slab foundation, drawings also include crawl space foundation

### Price Code B

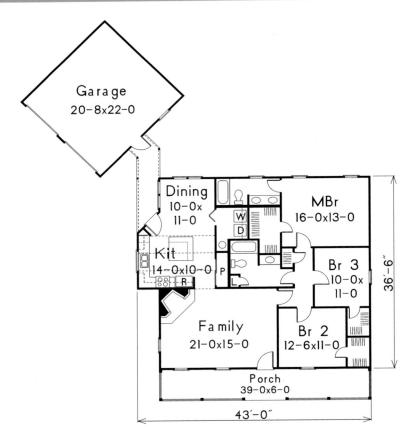

14

**MENARDS®**

*Dogwood*

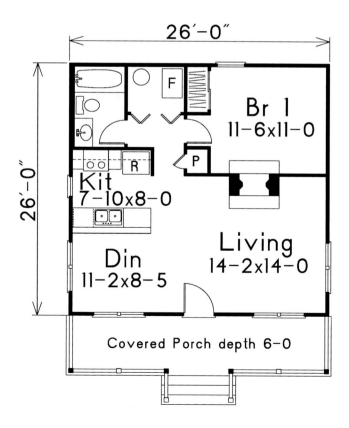

26'-0"

26'-0"

**Br 1**
11-6x11-0

**F**

**P**

**R**

**Kit**
7-10x8-0

**Din**
11-2x8-5

**Living**
14-2x14-0

Covered Porch depth 6-0

## Small And Cozy Cabin

676 total square feet of living area

### Special features

- See-through fireplace between bedroom and living area adds character
- Combined dining and living areas create an open feeling
- Full-length front covered porch is perfect for enjoying the outdoors
- Additional storage is available in the utility room
- 2" x 6" exterior walls available, please order plan #M03-058D-0074
- 1 bedroom, 1 bath
- Crawl space foundation

### Price Code AAA

**To order this plan, visit the Menards Building Materials Desk.**

## Summerview

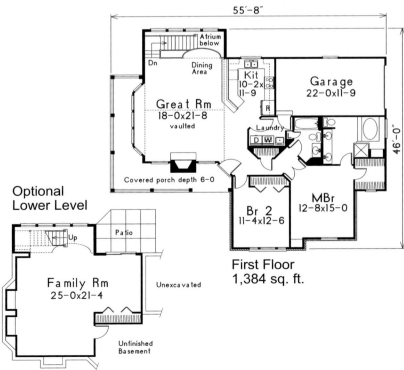

Rear View

# Tranquility Of An Atrium Cottage

1,384 total square feet of living area

### Special features

- Wrap-around country porch for peaceful evenings
- Vaulted great room enjoys a large bay window, stone fireplace, pass-through kitchen and awesome rear views through an atrium window wall
- Master bedroom features a double-door entry, walk-in closet and a fabulous bath
- Atrium opens to 611 square feet of optional living area below
- 2 bedrooms, 2 baths, 1-car side entry garage
- Walk-out basement foundation

## Price Code B

**Optional Lower Level**

Family Rm
25-0x21-4

Patio

Up

Unexcavated

Unfinished Basement

First Floor
1,384 sq. ft.

55'-8"

46'-0"

Atrium below

Dn

Dining Area

Kit
10-2x 11-9

Garage
22-0x11-9

Great Rm
18-0x21-8
vaulted

Laundry

D W

Covered porch depth 6-0

MBr
12-8x15-0

Br 2
11-4x12-6

**To order this plan, visit the Menards Building Materials Desk.**

*Waverly*

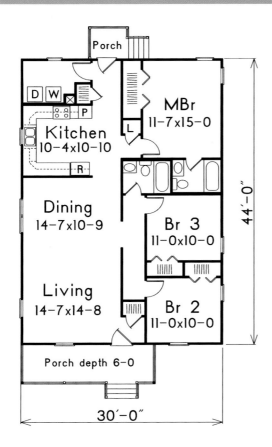

## Gabled, Covered Front Porch

1,320 total square feet of living area

### Special features

- Functional U-shaped kitchen features a pantry
- Large living and dining areas join to create an open atmosphere
- Secluded master bedroom includes a private full bath
- Covered front porch opens into a large living area with a convenient coat closet
- Utility/laundry room is located near the kitchen
- 3 bedrooms, 2 baths
- Crawl space foundation

## Price Code A

**To order this plan, visit the Menards Building Materials Desk.**

*Rosewind*

## Year-Round Or Weekend Getaway Home

1,339 total square feet of living area

### Special features

- Full-length covered porch enhances front facade
- Vaulted ceiling and stone fireplace add drama to the family room
- Walk-in closets in the bedrooms provide ample storage space
- Combined kitchen/dining area adjoins the family room for the perfect entertaining space
- 2" x 6" exterior walls available, please order plan #M03-058D-0072
- 3 bedrooms, 2 1/2 baths
- Crawl space foundation

### Price Code A

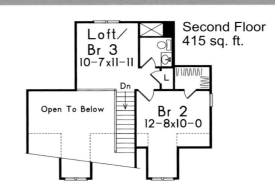

Second Floor
415 sq. ft.

Loft/Br 3
10-7x11-11

Br 2
12-8x10-0

Open To Below

Dn

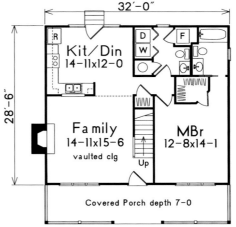

First Floor
924 sq. ft.

32'-0"

28'-6"

Kit/Din
14-11x12-0

Family
14-11x15-6
vaulted clg

MBr
12-8x14-1

Up

Covered Porch depth 7-0

**To order this plan, visit the Menards Building Materials Desk.**

*Bridgeport*

Second Floor
537 sq. ft.

Br 3
11-0x12-0

Br 2
11-0x13-0

Dn

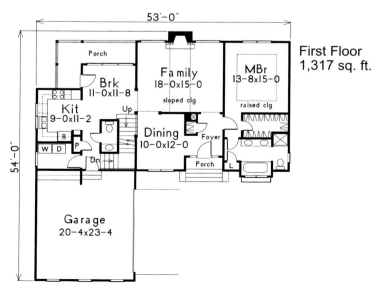

First Floor
1,317 sq. ft.

53'-0"

54'-0"

Porch

Brk
11-0x11-8

Kit
9-0x11-2

Family
18-0x15-0
sloped clg

MBr
13-8x15-0
raised clg

Up

Dining
10-0x12-0

Foyer

Dn

Porch

W D P R

Garage
20-4x23-4

## Stucco And Stone Add Charm To Facade

1,854 total square feet of living area

### Special features

- Front entrance is enhanced by arched transom windows and rustic stone
- Isolated master bedroom includes a dressing area and walk-in closet
- Family room features a high sloped ceiling and large fireplace
- Breakfast area accesses the covered rear porch
- 3 bedrooms, 2 1/2 baths, 2-car side entry garage
- Basement foundation

### Price Code D

**To order this plan, visit the Menards Building Materials Desk.**

# Plan #M03-053D-0030

**MENARDS**®

*Redfield*

## Quaint Exterior, Full Front Porch

1,657 total square feet of living area

### Special features

- Stylish pass-through between living and dining areas
- Master bedroom is secluded from the living area for privacy
- Large windows in the breakfast and dining areas create a bright and cheerful atmosphere
- 3 bedrooms, 2 1/2 baths, 2-car drive under garage
- Basement foundation

### Price Code B

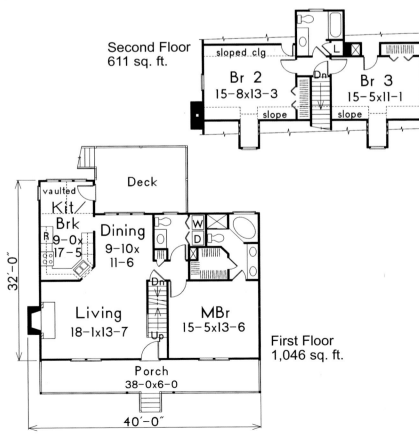

Second Floor
611 sq. ft.

sloped clg

Br 2
15-8x13-3

L

Dn

Br 3
15-5x11-1

slope          slope

Deck

vaulted

Kit/
Brk
R  9-0x
17-5

Dining
9-10x
11-6

W
D

32'-0"

Dn

Living
18-1x13-7

Up

MBr
15-5x13-6

First Floor
1,046 sq. ft.

Porch
38-0x6-0

40'-0"

20

**To order this plan, visit the Menards Building Materials Desk.**

*Crosswood*

## Ideal For A Starter Home

800 total square feet of living area

### Special features

- Master bedroom has a walk-in closet and private access to the bath
- Large living room features a handy coat closet
- Kitchen includes side entrance, closet and convenient laundry area
- 2 bedrooms, 1 bath
- Crawl space foundation, drawings also include basement foundation

### Price Code AAA

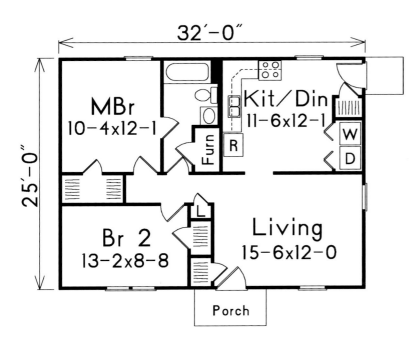

**To order this plan, visit the Menards Building Materials Desk.**

**MENARDS**®

*Stonehurst*

## Charming Country Styling In This Ranch

1,600 total square feet of living area

### Special features

- Energy efficient home with 2" x 6" exterior walls
- Impressive sunken living room features a massive stone fireplace and 16' vaulted ceiling
- The dining room is conveniently located next to the kitchen and divided for privacy
- Special amenities include a sewing room, glass shelves in the kitchen, a grand master bath and a large utility area
- 3 bedrooms, 2 baths, 2-car side entry garage
- Slab foundation, drawings also include crawl space and basement foundations

### Price Code C

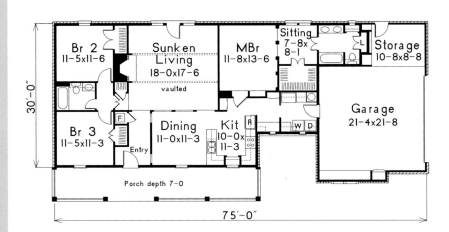

To order this plan, visit the **Menards Building Materials Desk.**

**Rear View**

*Sausalito*

## Ideal Home For Lake, Mountain Or Seaside

1,711 total square feet of living area

### Special features

- Entry leads to a vaulted great room with exposed beams, two-story window wall, fireplace, wet bar and balcony
- Bayed breakfast room shares the fireplace and joins a sun-drenched kitchen and deck
- Vaulted first floor master bedroom features a double-door entry, two closets and bookshelves
- Spiral stairs and a balcony dramatize the loft that doubles as a spacious second bedroom
- 2 bedrooms, 2 1/2 baths
- Basement foundation

### Price Code B

**Second Floor**
397 sq. ft.

open to below

plant shelf

Dn

Loft/Br 2
19-3x12-0
vaulted

MBr
below

N

**First Floor**
1,314 sq. ft.

40'-0"

Deck

34'-0"

Great Rm
19-3x18-6
vaulted

Kit/Brk
17-3x
14-0

P R

Up

Dn

Entry

MBr
13-7x14-7
vaulted

Porch

**To order this plan, visit the Menards Building Materials Desk.**

23

## Wheatland

## Surrounding Porch For Country Views

1,428 total square feet of living area

### Special features

- Large vaulted family room opens to the dining area and kitchen with breakfast bar
- First floor master bedroom offers a large bath, walk-in closet and nearby laundry facilities
- A spacious loft/bedroom #3 overlooking the family room and an additional bedroom and bath complement the second floor
- 2" x 6" exterior walls available, please order plan #M03-058D-0080
- 3 bedrooms, 2 baths
- Basement foundation

### Price Code A

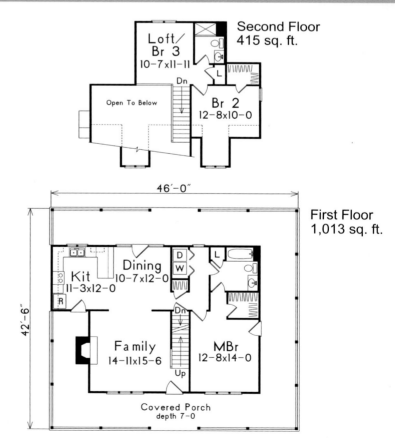

Second Floor
415 sq. ft.

Loft/
Br 3
10-7x11-11

Open To Below

Br 2
12-8x10-0

Dn

46'-0"

First Floor
1,013 sq. ft.

42'-6"

Kit
11-3x12-0

Dining
10-7x12-0

Family
14-11x15-6

MBr
12-8x14-0

Dn

Up

Covered Porch
depth 7-0

**To order this plan, visit the Menards Building Materials Desk.**

*Chalet*

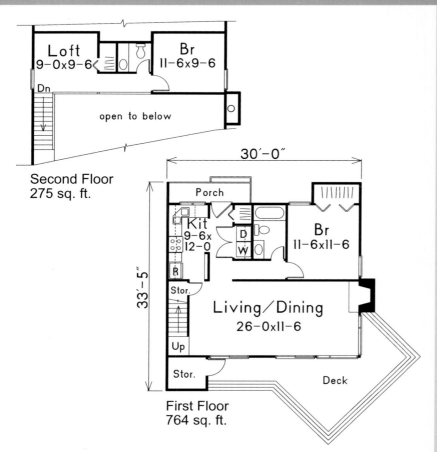

Loft
9-0x9-6

Br
11-6x9-6

Dn

open to below

**Second Floor**
**275 sq. ft.**

30'-0"

Porch

Kit
9-6x
12-0

D
W

Br
11-6x11-6

33'-5"

Stor.

Up

Living/Dining
26-0x11-6

Stor.

Deck

**First Floor**
**764 sq. ft.**

## A Vacation Home For All Seasons

1,039 total square feet of living area

### Special features

- Cathedral construction provides the maximum in living area openness
- Expansive glass viewing walls
- Two decks, front and back
- Charming second story loft arrangement
- Simple, low-maintenance construction
- 2 bedrooms, 1 1/2 baths
- Crawl space foundation

### Price Code AA

**To order this plan, visit the Menards Building Materials Desk.**

*Westrose*

## Cozy Front Porch Welcomes Guests

1,393 total square feet of living area

### Special features

- L-shaped kitchen features a walk-in pantry, island cooktop and is convenient to the laundry room and dining area
- Master bedroom features a large walk-in closet and private bath with separate tub and shower
- Convenient storage/coat closet in hall
- View to the patio from the dining area
- 3 bedrooms, 2 baths, 2-car detached garage
- Crawl space foundation, drawings also include slab foundation

### Price Code B

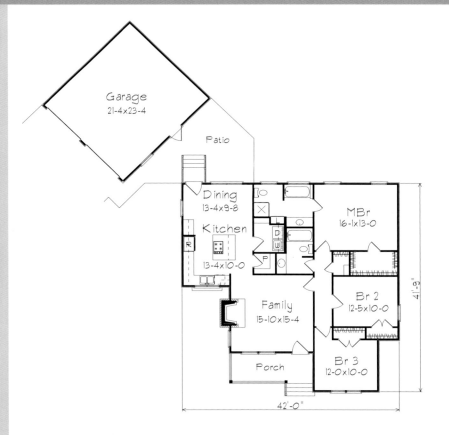

Garage
21-4x23-4

Patio

Dining
13-4x9-8

Kitchen
13-4x10-0

MBr
16-1x13-0

Family
15-10x15-4

Br 2
12-5x10-0

Porch

Br 3
12-0x10-0

41'-9"

42'-0"

*Glen Ellen*

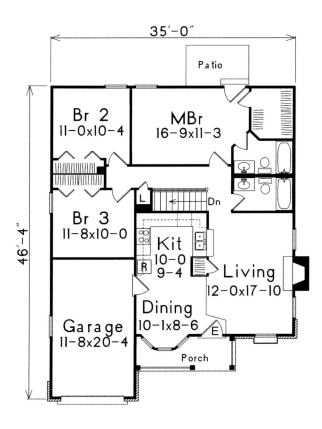

## Country Charm For A Small Lot

1,169 total square feet of living area

### Special features

- Front facade features a distinctive country appeal
- Living room enjoys a wood-burning fireplace and pass-through to kitchen
- A stylish U-shaped kitchen offers an abundance of cabinet and counter-space with view to living room
- A large walk-in closet, access to rear patio and private bath are many features of the master bedroom
- 3 bedrooms, 2 baths, 1-car garage
- Basement foundation

### Price Code AA

**To order this plan, visit the Menards Building Materials Desk.**

*Grass Roots 1*

## Open Living Space Creates Comfortable Atmosphere

1,000 total square feet of living area

### Special features

- Bath includes convenient closeted laundry area
- Master bedroom includes double closets and private access to the bath
- The foyer features a handy coat closet
- L-shaped kitchen provides easy access outdoors
- 3 bedrooms, 1 bath
- Crawl space foundation, drawings also include basement and slab foundations

### Price Code AA

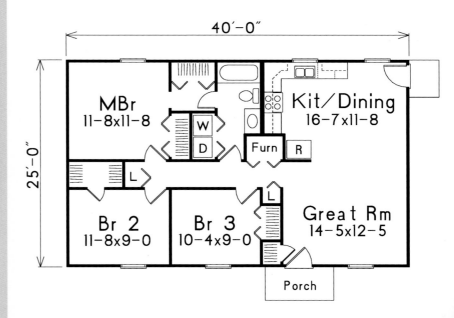

**To order this plan, visit the Menards Building Materials Desk.**

**MENARDS**®

*Greenview*

Second Floor
686 sq. ft.

Br 3
11-0x11-6

Loft/
Br 4
10-8x11-6

Br 2
14-6x10-6

Dn

open to below

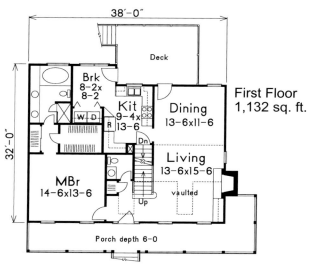

38'-0"

Deck

Brk
8-2x
8-2

Kit
9-4x
13-6

Dining
13-6x11-6

W D

R

32'-0"

Dn

First Floor
1,132 sq. ft.

Living
13-6x15-6

MBr
14-6x13-6

vaulted

Up

Porch depth 6-0

## Dormers Accent Country Home

1,818 total square feet of living area

### Special features

- Breakfast room is tucked behind the kitchen and has a laundry closet and deck access
- Living and dining areas share a vaulted ceiling and fireplace
- Master bedroom has two closets, a large double-bowl vanity and a separate tub and shower
- Large front porch wraps around the home
- 4 bedrooms, 2 1/2 baths, 2-car drive under garage
- Basement foundation

### Price Code C

**To order this plan, visit the Menards Building Materials Desk.**

*Fairmont*

## Four Bedroom Home For A Narrow Lot

1,452 total square feet of living area

### Special features

- A large living room features a cozy corner fireplace, bayed dining area and access from the entry with a guest closet
- Forward master bedroom enjoys having its own bath and linen closet
- Three additional bedrooms share a bath with a double-bowl vanity
- 4 bedrooms, 2 baths
- Basement foundation

### Price Code A

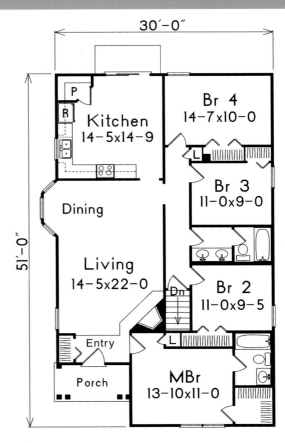

**To order this plan, visit the Menards Building Materials Desk.**

*Newburgh*

## Second Floor
1,050 sq. ft.

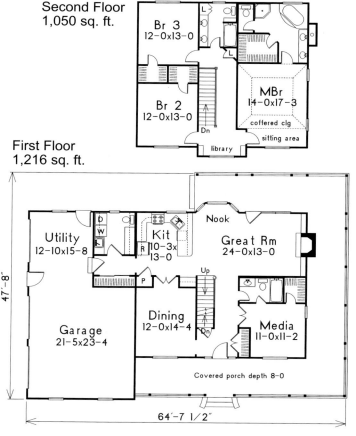

Br 3
12-0x13-0

Br 2
12-0x13-0

MBr
14-0x17-3

coffered clg

sitting area

library

## First Floor
1,216 sq. ft.

Utility
12-10x15-8

Kit
10-3x
13-0

Nook

Great Rm
24-0x13-0

Dining
12-0x14-4

Media
11-0x11-2

Garage
21-5x23-4

Up

Dn

P

D

W

R

47'-8"

64'-7 1/2"

Covered porch depth 8-0

## Wrap-Around Porch Creates A Comfortable Feel

2,266 total square feet of living area

### Special features

- Great room includes a fireplace flanked by built-in bookshelves and dining nook with bay window
- Unique media room includes a double-door entrance, walk-in closet and access to a full bath
- Master bedroom has a lovely sitting area and private bath with a walk-in closet, step-up tub and double vanity
- 3 bedrooms, 3 1/2 baths, 2-car side entry garage
- Basement foundation, drawings also include crawl space foundation

### Price Code D

**To order this plan, visit the Menards Building Materials Desk.**

# Plan #M03-058D-0012

*Walnut Grove*

## Flexible Layout For Various Uses

1,143 total square feet of living area

### Special features

- Enormous stone fireplace in the family room adds warmth and character
- Spacious kitchen with breakfast bar overlooks the family room
- Separate dining area is great for entertaining
- Vaulted family room and kitchen create an open atmosphere
- 2" x 6" exterior walls available, please order plan #M03-058D-0075
- 2 bedrooms, 1 bath
- Crawl space foundation

**Price Code AA**

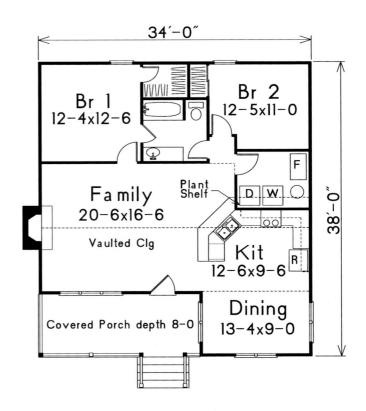

34'-0"

Br 1
12-4x12-6

Br 2
12-5x11-0

F

Plant Shelf

D | W

Family
20-6x16-6

Vaulted Clg

Kit
12-6x9-6

R

38'-0"

Covered Porch depth 8-0

Dining
13-4x9-0

**To order this plan, visit the Menards Building Materials Desk.**

*Harrison*

## Large Front Porch Adds Welcoming Appeal

829 total square feet of living area

### Special features

- U-shaped kitchen opens into living area by a 42" high counter
- Oversized bay window and French door accent dining room
- Gathering space is created by the large living room
- Convenient utility room and linen closet
- 1 bedroom, 1 bath
- Slab foundation

### Price Code AAA

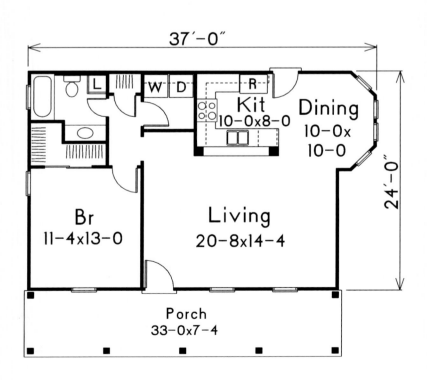

37'-0"

Kit
10-0x8-0

Dining
10-0x
10-0

24'-0"

Br
11-4x13-0

Living
20-8x14-4

Porch
33-0x7-4

*Pinebluff*

## Well-Designed Ranch With Wrap-Around Porch

1,823 total square feet of living area

### Special features

- Vaulted living room is spacious and easily accesses the dining area
- The master bedroom boasts a tray ceiling, large walk-in closet and a private bath with a corner whirlpool tub
- Cheerful dining area is convenient to the U-shaped kitchen and also enjoys patio access
- Centrally located laundry room connects the garage to the living areas
- 3 bedrooms, 2 baths, 2-car garage
- Basement foundation

### Price Code C

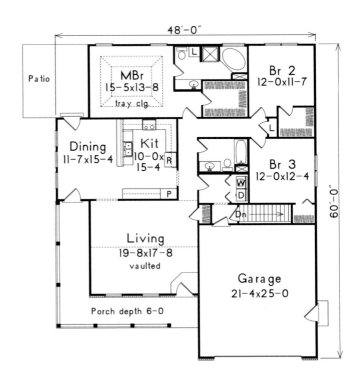

34

**To order this plan, visit the Menards Building Materials Desk.**

**MENARDS**®

*Hillbriar*

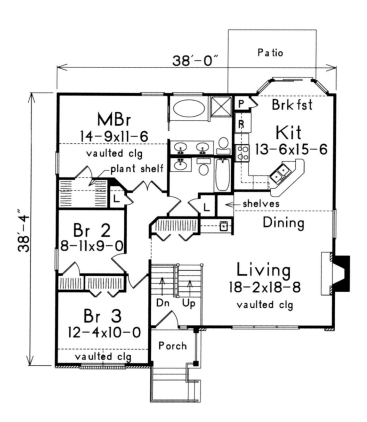

38′-0″

Patio

MBr
14-9x11-6
vaulted clg
plant shelf

Brk fst

Kit
13-6x15-6

38′-4″

Br 2
8-11x9-0

shelves

Dining

Living
18-2x18-8
vaulted clg

Dn  Up

Br 3
12-4x10-0
vaulted clg

Porch

## Distinctive Home For Sloping Terrain

1,340 total square feet of living area

### Special features

- Grand-sized vaulted living and dining rooms offer fireplace, wet bar and breakfast counter open to a spacious kitchen
- Vaulted master bedroom features a double-door entry, walk-in closet and an elegant bath
- Basement includes a huge two-car garage and space for a bedroom/bath expansion
- 3 bedrooms, 2 baths, 2-car drive under garage with storage area
- Basement foundation

### Price Code A

**To order this plan, visit the Menards Building Materials Desk.**

*Woodbridge*

## Open Living Area

1,154 total square feet of living area

### Special features

- U-shaped kitchen features a large breakfast bar and handy laundry area
- Private second floor bedrooms share a half bath
- Large living/dining area opens to deck
- 3 bedrooms, 1 1/2 baths
- Crawl space foundation, drawings also include slab foundation

### Price Code AA

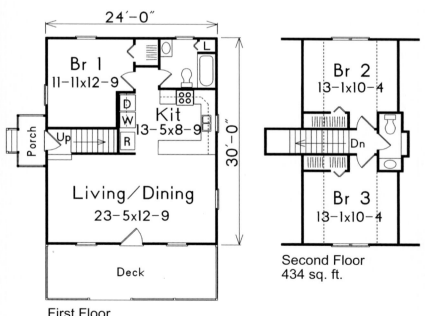

24'-0"

30'-0"

Br 1
11–11x12–9

Kit
13–5x8–9

Porch

Up

D
W
R

Living/Dining
23–5x12–9

Deck

First Floor
720 sq. ft.

Br 2
13–1x10–4

Dn

Br 3
13–1x10–4

Second Floor
434 sq. ft.

**To order this plan, visit the Menards Building Materials Desk.**

Jonesboro

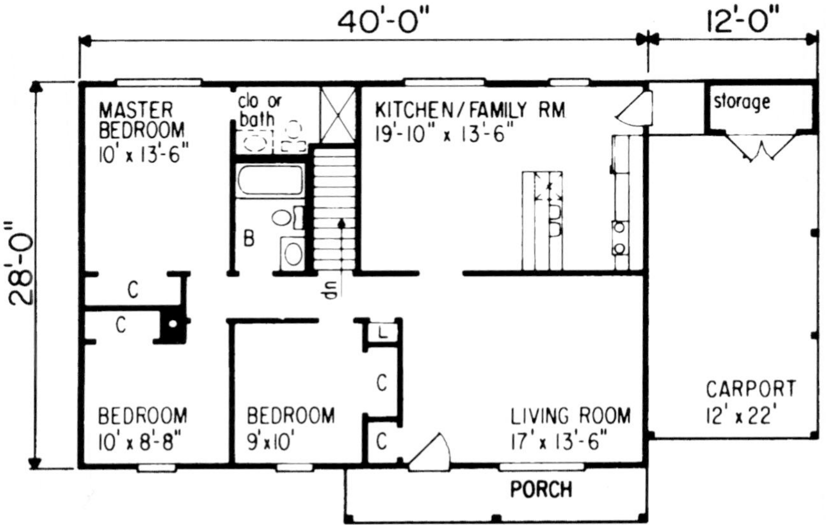
40'-0"
12'-0"
28'-0"
MASTER BEDROOM 10' x 13'-6"
clo or bath
B
KITCHEN/FAMILY RM 19'-10" x 13'-6"
storage
C
C
dn
L
C
C
BEDROOM 10' x 8'-8"
BEDROOM 9'x10'
LIVING ROOM 17' x 13'-6"
CARPORT 12' x 22'
PORCH

## Lovely Inviting Covered Porch

1,120 total square feet of living area

**Special features**

- Kitchen/family room creates a useful spacious area
- Rustic, colonial design is perfect for many surroundings
- Oversized living room is ideal for entertaining
- Carport includes a functional storage area
- 3 bedrooms, 2 baths, 1-car carport
- Basement foundation, drawings also include crawl space and slab foundations

**Price Code AA**

## Springdale

## Stylish Retreat For A Narrow Lot

1,084 total square feet of living area

### Special features

- Delightful country porch for quiet evenings
- The living room offers a front feature window which invites the sun and includes a fireplace and dining area with private patio
- The U-shaped kitchen features lots of cabinets and a bayed breakfast room with built-in pantry
- Both bedrooms have walk-in closets and access to their own bath
- 2 bedrooms, 2 baths
- Basement foundation

### Price Code AA

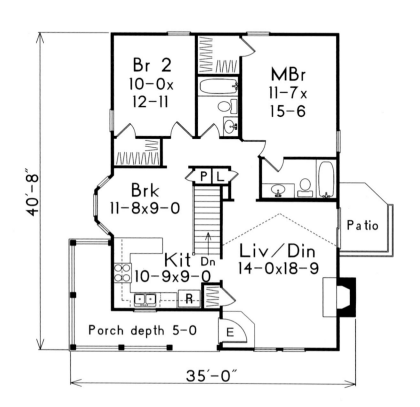

Br 2
10-0x 12-11

MBr
11-7x 15-6

Brk
11-8x9-0

Kit
10-9x9-0

Liv/Din
14-0x18-9

Patio

Porch depth 5-0

40'-8"

35'-0"

**To order this plan, visit the Menards Building Materials Desk.**

*Foxland*

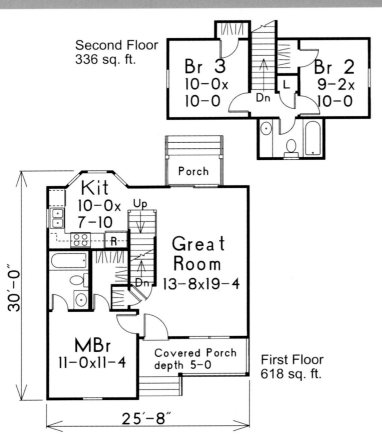

Second Floor
336 sq. ft.

**Br 3**
10-0x
10-0

Dn

L

**Br 2**
9-2x
10-0

Porch

**Kit**
10-0x
7-10

Up

R

**Great Room**
13-8x19-4

Dn

30'-0"

**MBr**
11-0x11-4

Covered Porch
depth 5-0

First Floor
618 sq. ft.

25'-8"

## Dormer And Covered Porch Add To Country Charm

954 total square feet of living area

### Special features

- Kitchen has a cozy bayed eating area
- Master bedroom has a walk-in closet and private bath
- Large great room has access to the back porch
- Convenient coat closet is near the front entry
- 3 bedrooms, 2 baths
- Basement foundation

### Price Code AA

**To order this plan, visit the Menards Building Materials Desk.**

*El Dorado*

## Floor-To-Ceiling Window Expands Compact Two-Story

1,246 total square feet of living area

### Special features

- Corner living room window adds openness and light
- Out-of-the-way kitchen with dining area accesses the outdoors
- Private first floor master bedroom has a corner window
- Large walk-in closet is located in bedroom #3
- Easily built perimeter allows economical construction
- 3 bedrooms, 2 baths, 2-car garage
- Basement foundation

### Price Code A

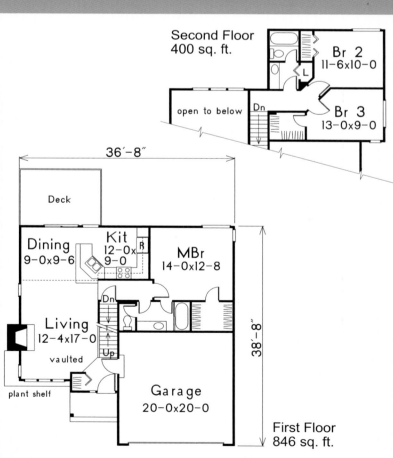

Second Floor 400 sq. ft.

Br 2 11-6x10-0

open to below | Dn

Br 3 13-0x9-0

36'-8"

Deck

Dining 9-0x9-6

Kit 12-0x 9-0

MBr 14-0x12-8

Living 12-4x17-0

vaulted

plant shelf

Garage 20-0x20-0

38'-8"

First Floor 846 sq. ft.

**To order this plan, visit the Menards Building Materials Desk.**

*Antonia*

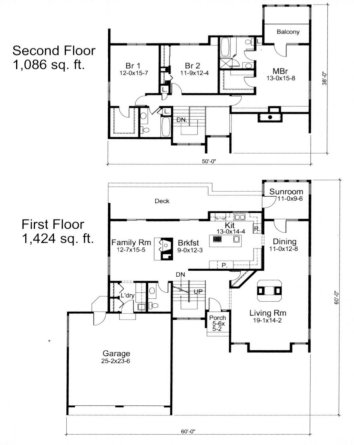

Second Floor
1,086 sq. ft.

Balcony

Br 1
12-0x15-7

Br 2
11-9x12-4

MBr
13-0x15-8

38'-0"

DN.

50'-0"

First Floor
1,424 sq. ft.

Deck

Sunroom
11-0x9-6

Kit
13-0x14-4

Family Rm
12-7x15-5

Brkfst
9-0x12-3

Dining
11-0x12-8

R.

P.

DN

L'dry

UP

Porch
5-6x
5-2

Living Rm
19-1x14-2

60'-0"

Garage
25-2x23-6

60'-0"

## Contemporary Design

2,510 total square feet of living area

### Special features

- Energy efficient home with 2" x 6" exterior walls
- Both formal and informal living spaces are graced with stylish fireplaces
- Enjoy the large deck and sunroom located off the dining room
- All of the bedrooms are located on the second floor, including the master suite complete with a private balcony
- 3 bedrooms, 2 1/2 baths, 2-car garage
- Basement foundation

### Price Code E

**To order this plan, visit the Menards Building Materials Desk.**

*Auburn*

## Breezeway Joins Living Space With Garage

1,874 total square feet of living area

### Special features

- 9' ceilings throughout the first floor
- Two-story foyer opens into the large family room with fireplace
- First floor master bedroom includes a private bath with tub and shower
- 4 bedrooms, 2 1/2 baths, 2-car garage
- Basement foundation, drawings also include slab foundation

### Price Code C

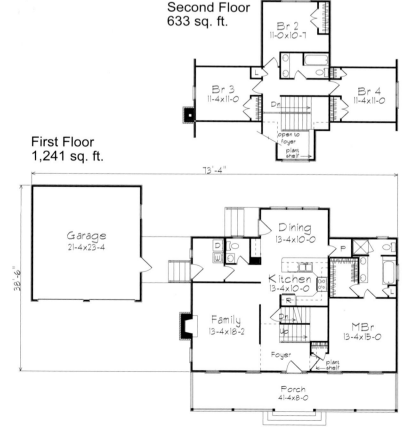

Second Floor
633 sq. ft.

Br 2
11-0x10-7

Br 3
11-4x11-0

Br 4
11-4x11-0

open to foyer

plant shelf

First Floor
1,241 sq. ft.

73'-4"

38'-6"

Garage
21-4x23-4

Dining
13-4x10-0

Kitchen
13-4x10-0

Family
13-4x18-2

MBr
13-4x15-0

Foyer

plant shelf

Porch
41-4x8-0

**To order this plan, visit the Menards Building Materials Desk.**

# Plan #M03-001D-0085

*Highlander*

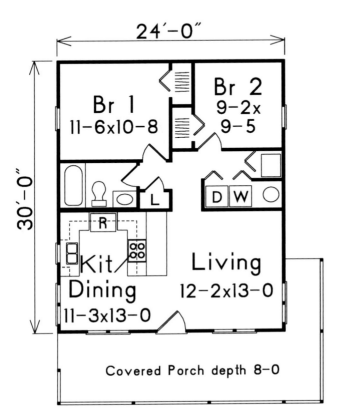

24'-0"

Br 1
11-6x10-8

Br 2
9-2x
9-5

30'-0"

L

D W

Kit
Dining
11-3x13-0

R

Living
12-2x13-0

Covered Porch depth 8-0

## Designed For Comfort And Utility

720 total square feet of living area

### Special features

- Abundant windows in living and dining rooms provide generous sunlight
- Secluded laundry area has a handy storage closet
- U-shaped kitchen with large breakfast bar opens into living area
- Large covered deck offers plenty of outdoor living space
- 2 bedrooms, 1 bath
- Crawl space foundation, drawings also include slab foundation

### Price Code AAA

**To order this plan, visit the Menards Building Materials Desk.**

*Summerpath*

## Country Cottage Offers Large Vaulted Living Space

962 total square feet of living area

### Special features

- Both the kitchen and family room share warmth from the fireplace
- Charming facade features a covered porch on one side, screened porch on the other and attractive planter boxes
- L-shaped kitchen boasts a convenient pantry
- 2 bedrooms, 1 bath
- Crawl space foundation

### Price Code AA

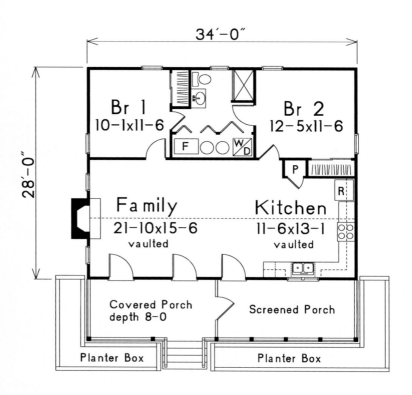

**To order this plan, visit the Menards Building Materials Desk.**

*Breezewood*

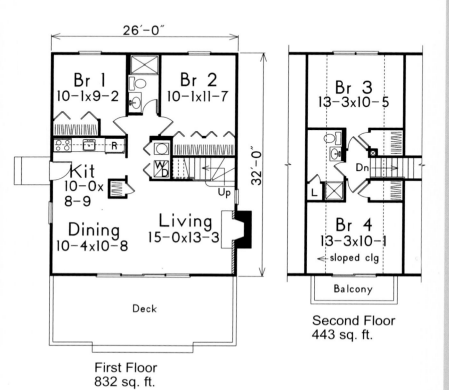

First Floor
832 sq. ft.

Second Floor
443 sq. ft.

## Rustic Haven

1,275 total square feet of living area

### Special features

- Wall shingles and a stone veneer fireplace all fashion an irresistible rustic appeal
- Living area features a fireplace and opens to an efficient kitchen
- Two bedrooms on the second floor
- 4 bedrooms, 2 baths
- Basement foundation, drawings also include crawl space and slab foundations

### Price Code A

**To order this plan, visit the Menards Building Materials Desk.**

**MENARDS**®

*Parkhill*

## Three-Car Apartment Garage With Country Flair

**929 total square feet of living area**

### Special features

- Spacious living room with dining area has access to 8' x 12' deck through glass sliding doors
- Splendid U-shaped kitchen features a breakfast bar, oval window above sink and impressive cabinet storage
- Master bedroom enjoys a walk-in closet and large elliptical feature window
- Laundry, storage closet and mechanical space are located off the first floor garage
- 2 bedrooms, 1 bath, 3-car side entry garage
- Slab foundation

### Price Code AA

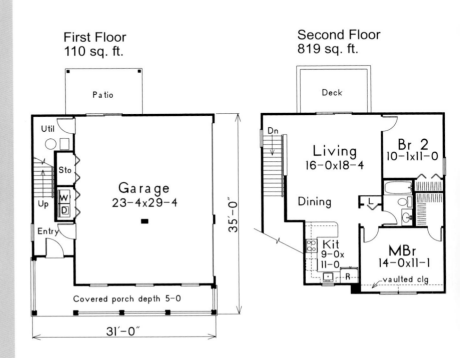

First Floor
110 sq. ft.

Second Floor
819 sq. ft.

**To order this plan, visit the Menards Building Materials Desk.**

*Dover*

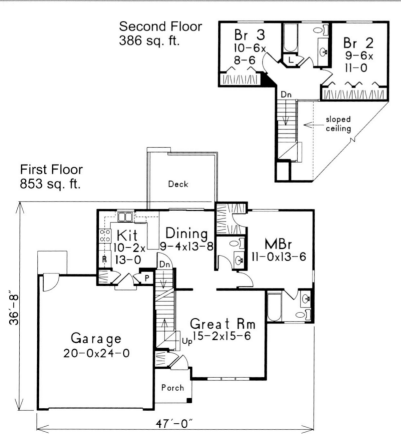

Second Floor
386 sq. ft.

Br 3
10-6x
8-6

Br 2
9-6x
11-0

Dn

sloped
ceiling

First Floor
853 sq. ft.

Deck

Kit
10-2x
13-0

Dining
9-4x13-8

MBr
11-0x13-6

Dn

36'-8"

Garage
20-0x24-0

Great Rm
15-2x15-6
Up

Porch

47'-0"

## Gables Accent
## This Home

1,239 total square feet of living area

### Special features

- Master bedroom has a private bath and walk-in closet
- Convenient coat closet and pantry are located near the garage entrance
- Dining area accesses the deck
- Stairway with sloped ceiling creates an open atmosphere in the great room
- 3 bedrooms, 2 1/2 baths, 2-car garage
- Basement foundation

### Price Code A

**To order this plan, visit the Menards Building Materials Desk.**

*Grandview*

## Spacious A-Frame

1,769 total square feet of living area

### Special features

- Living room boasts an elegant cathedral ceiling and fireplace
- U-shaped kitchen and dining area combine for easy living
- Secondary bedrooms include double closets
- Secluded master bedroom features a sloped ceiling, large walk-in closet and private bath
- 2" x 6" exterior walls available, please order plan #M03-001D-0124
- 3 bedrooms, 2 baths
- Basement foundation, drawings also include crawl space and slab foundations

### Price Code B

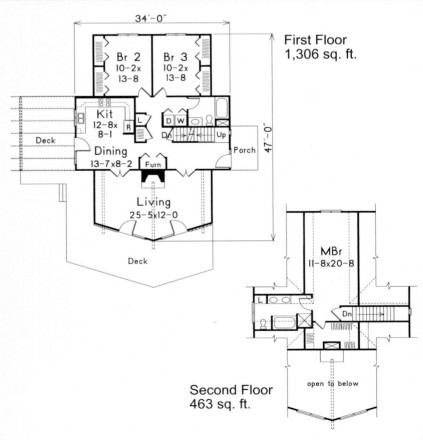

First Floor
1,306 sq. ft.

Second Floor
463 sq. ft.

**To order this plan, visit the Menards Building Materials Desk.**

*Ridgeland*

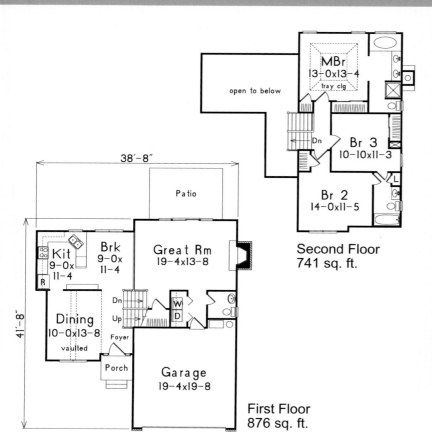

**Second Floor**
**741 sq. ft.**

**First Floor**
**876 sq. ft.**

## Efficient Layout In This Multi-Level Home

1,617 total square feet of living area

### Special features

- Kitchen and breakfast area overlook the great room with fireplace
- Formal dining room features a vaulted ceiling and an elegant circle-top window
- All bedrooms are located on the second floor for privacy
- 3 bedrooms, 2 1/2 baths, 2-car garage
- Partial crawl space/slab foundation

**Price Code B**

**To order this plan, visit the Menards Building Materials Desk.**

*Pagehurst*

## Old-Fashioned Comfort And Privacy

1,772 total square feet of living area

### Special features

- Extended porches in front and rear provide a charming touch
- Large bay windows lend distinction to the dining room and bedroom #3
- Efficient U-shaped kitchen
- Master bedroom includes two walk-in closets
- Full corner fireplace in family room
- 3 bedrooms, 2 baths, 2-car detached garage
- Slab foundation, drawings also include crawl space foundation

### Price Code C

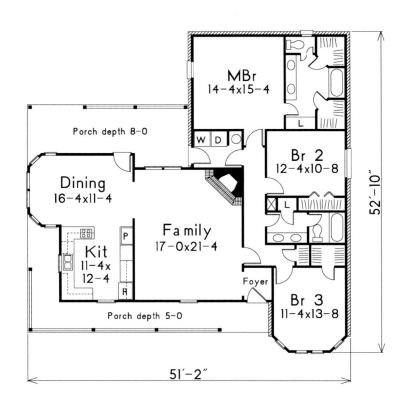

**To order this plan, visit the Menards Building Materials Desk.**

*Sunmist*

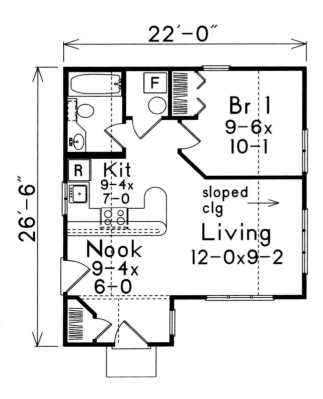

## Graciously Designed Refuge

527 total square feet of living area

### Special features

- Cleverly arranged home has it all
- Foyer spills into the dining nook with access to side views
- An excellent kitchen offers a long breakfast bar and borders the living room with a free-standing fireplace
- A cozy bedroom has a full bath just across the hall
- 1 bedroom, 1 bath
- Crawl space foundation

### Price Code AAA

*Lexburg*

## Open Layout Ensures Easy Living

976 total square feet of living area

### Special features

■ Cozy front porch opens into the large living room
■ Convenient half bath is located on the first floor
■ All bedrooms are located on the second floor for privacy
■ Dining room has access to the outdoors
■ 3 bedrooms, 1 1/2 baths
■ Basement foundation

### Price Code AA

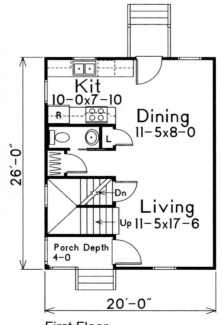

First Floor
488 sq. ft.

Second Floor
488 sq. ft.

**To order this plan, visit the Menards Building Materials Desk.**

*Shadywood*

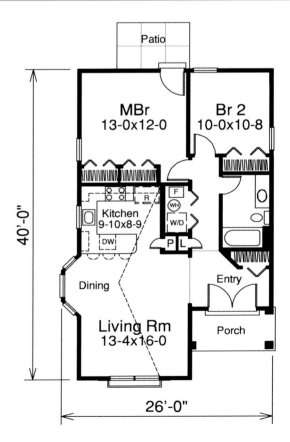

## Ideal Cottage Home For A Narrow Lot

882 total square feet of living area

### Special features

- An inviting porch and entry lure you into this warm and cozy home
- Living room features a vaulted ceiling, bayed dining area and is open to a well-equipped U-shaped kitchen
- The master bedroom has two separate closets and an access door to the rear patio
- 2 bedrooms, 1 bath
- Crawl space foundation, drawings also include slab and basement foundations

### Price Code AAA

*Ashland*

# Layout Features All The Essentials For Comfortable Living

1,344 total square feet of living area

### Special features

- Kitchen has side entry, laundry area, pantry and joins the family/dining area
- Master bedroom includes a private bath
- Linen and storage closets in hall
- Covered porch opens to the spacious living room with a handy coat closet
- 3 bedrooms, 2 baths
- Crawl space foundation, drawings also include basement and slab foundations

### Price Code A

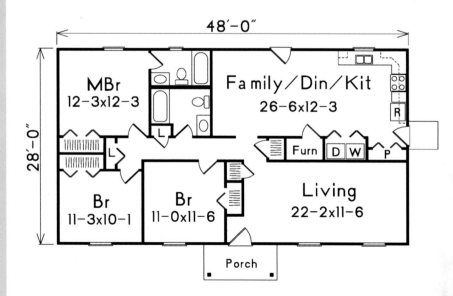

**To order this plan, visit the Menards Building Materials Desk.**

# Plan #M03-008D-0140

*Greeley*

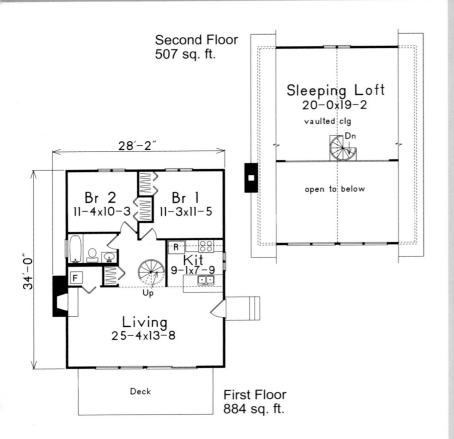

Second Floor
507 sq. ft.

**Sleeping Loft**
20-0x19-2
vaulted clg

Dn

open to below

28'-2"

**Br 2**
11-4x10-3

**Br 1**
11-3x11-5

**Kit**
9-1x7-9

R

F

34'-0"

Up

**Living**
25-4x13-8

Deck

First Floor
884 sq. ft.

## Cozy Vacation Retreat

1,391 total square feet of living area

### Special features

- Large living room with masonry fireplace features a soaring vaulted ceiling
- A spiral staircase in the hall leads to a huge loft area overlooking the living room below
- Two first floor bedrooms share a full bath
- 2 bedrooms, 1 bath
- Pier foundation, drawings also include crawl space foundation

### Price Code A

**To order this plan, visit the Menards Building Materials Desk.**

*Treebrooke*

## Country Kitchen Is Center Of Living Activities

1,556 total square feet of living area

### Special features

- A compact home with all the amenities
- Country kitchen combines practicality with access to other areas for eating and entertaining
- Two-way fireplace joins the dining and living areas
- Plant shelf and vaulted ceiling highlight the master bedroom
- 3 bedrooms, 2 1/2 baths, 2-car garage
- Basement foundation

### Price Code B

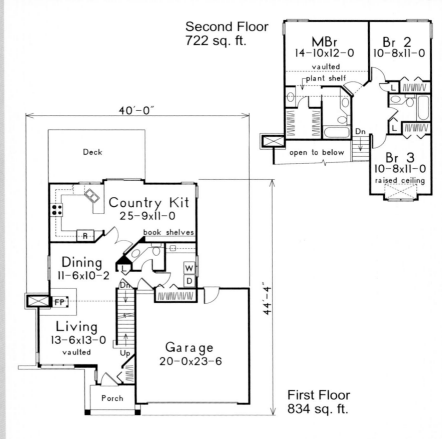

Second Floor
722 sq. ft.

MBr
14-10x12-0
vaulted
plant shelf

Br 2
10-8x11-0

open to below

Br 3
10-8x11-0
raised ceiling

Deck

40'-0"

Country Kit
25-9x11-0
book shelves

Dining
11-6x10-2

Living
13-6x13-0
vaulted

FP

44'-4"

Garage
20-0x23-6

Porch

First Floor
834 sq. ft.

**To order this plan, visit the Menards Building Materials Desk.**

**MENARDS**®

*Andover*

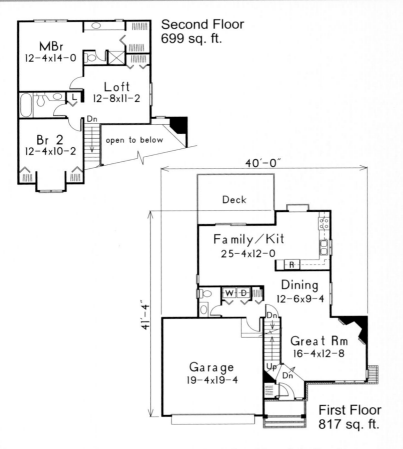

Second Floor
699 sq. ft.

MBr
12-4x14-0

Loft
12-8x11-2

Br 2
12-4x10-2

open to below

Dn

40'-0"

Deck

Family/Kit
25-4x12-0

Dining
12-6x9-4

W D

41'-4"

Dn

Great Rm
16-4x12-8

Garage
19-4x19-4

Up

Dn

First Floor
817 sq. ft.

## Contemporary Design For Open Family Living

1,516 total square feet of living area

### Special features

- All living and dining areas are interconnected for a spacious look and easy movement
- Covered entrance leads into sunken great room with a rugged corner fireplace
- Family kitchen combines practicality with access to other areas
- Second floor loft opens to rooms below and can convert to a third bedroom
- The dormer in bedroom #2 adds interest
- 2 bedrooms, 2 1/2 baths, 2-car garage
- Basement foundation

## Price Code B

**To order this plan, visit the Menards Building Materials Desk.**

*Princeton*

## Transom Windows Create Impressive Front Entry

1,800 total square feet of living area

### Special features

- Energy efficient home with 2" x 6" exterior walls
- Covered front and rear porches add outdoor living area
- 12' ceilings in the kitchen, breakfast area, dining and living rooms
- Private master bedroom features an expansive bath
- Side entry garage has two storage areas
- Pillared styling with brick and stucco exterior finish
- 3 bedrooms, 2 baths, 2-car side entry garage
- Crawl space foundation, drawings also include slab foundation

### Price Code D

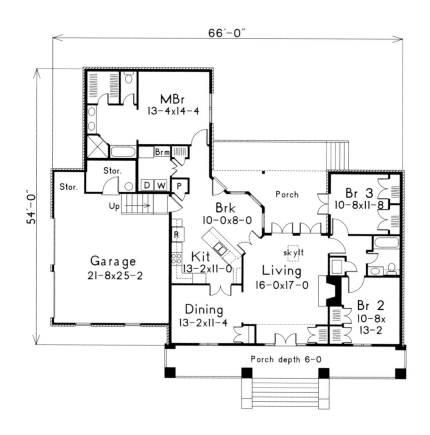

**To order this plan, visit the Menards Building Materials Desk.**

*Berrycreek*

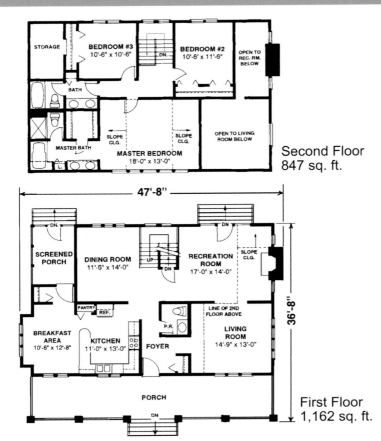

BEDROOM #3
10'-6" x 10'-6"

BEDROOM #2
10'-6" x 11'-6"

STORAGE

OPEN TO
REC. RM.
BELOW

DN.

BATH

MASTER BATH

SLOPE
CLG.

SLOPE
CLG.

OPEN TO LIVING
ROOM BELOW

MASTER BEDROOM
18'-0" x 13'-0"

**Second Floor
847 sq. ft.**

47'-8"

36'-8"

DN.

SCREENED
PORCH

DINING ROOM
11'-6" x 14'-0"

UP

DN.

RECREATION
ROOM
17'-0" x 14'-0"

SLOPE
CLG.

DN.

PANTRY
REF.

LINE OF 2ND
FLOOR ABOVE

P.R.

BREAKFAST
AREA
10'-6" x 12'-8"

KITCHEN
11'-0" x 13'-0"

FOYER

LIVING
ROOM
14'-9" x 13'-0"

PORCH

DN.

**First Floor
1,162 sq. ft.**

## Extra Amenities Enhance Living

2,009 total square feet of living area

### Special features

- Spacious master bedroom has a dramatic sloped ceiling and private bath with a double-bowl vanity and walk-in closet
- Bedroom #3 has an extra storage area behind the closet
- Versatile screened porch is ideal for entertaining year-round
- Sunny breakfast area is located near the kitchen and screened porch for convenience
- 3 bedrooms, 2 1/2 baths
- Basement foundation

### Price Code C

**To order this plan, visit the Menards Building Materials Desk.**

*Glenwood*

## Apartment Garage With Surprising Interior

632 total square feet of living area

### Special features

- Porch leads to a vaulted entry and stair with feature window, coat closet and access to garage/laundry
- Cozy living room offers a vaulted ceiling, fireplace, large palladian window and pass-through to kitchen
- A garden tub with arched window is part of a very roomy bath
- 1 bedroom, 1 bath, 2-car garage
- Slab foundation

### Price Code AAA

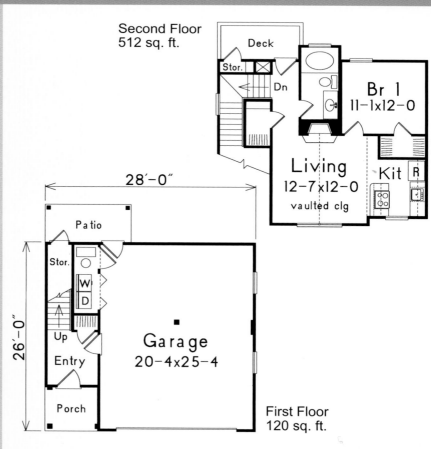

Second Floor
512 sq. ft.

Deck

Stor.

Dn

Br 1
11-1x12-0

Living
12-7x12-0
vaulted clg

Kit

R

28'-0"

26'-0"

Patio

Stor.

W
D

Up

Entry

Porch

Garage
20-4x25-4

First Floor
120 sq. ft.

**To order this plan, visit the Menards Building Materials Desk.**

**MENARDS**®

*Lakewood*

## Perfect Vacation Home

1,230 total square feet of living area

### Special features

- Spacious living room accesses huge deck
- Bedroom #3 features a balcony overlooking the deck
- Kitchen with dining area accesses the outdoors
- Washer and dryer are tucked under the stairs for space efficiency
- 3 bedrooms, 1 bath
- Crawl space foundation, drawings also include slab foundation

### Price Code A

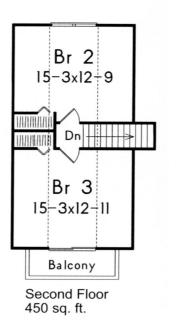

26'-0"

30'-0"

R

Br 1
9-2x
12-9

Kit
Dining
8-1x
16-6

D W W

Up

Living
25-5x12-11

Deck

**First Floor**
780 sq. ft.

Br 2
15-3x12-9

Dn

Br 3
15-3x12-11

Balcony

**Second Floor**
450 sq. ft.

*Haverhill*

## Cottage Style Is Appealing And Cozy

828 total square feet of living area

### Special features

- Vaulted ceiling in living area enhances space
- Convenient laundry room
- Sloped ceiling creates unique style in bedroom #2
- Efficient storage space under the stairs
- Covered entry porch provides a cozy sitting area and plenty of shade
- 2 bedrooms, 1 bath
- Crawl space foundation

### Price Code AAA

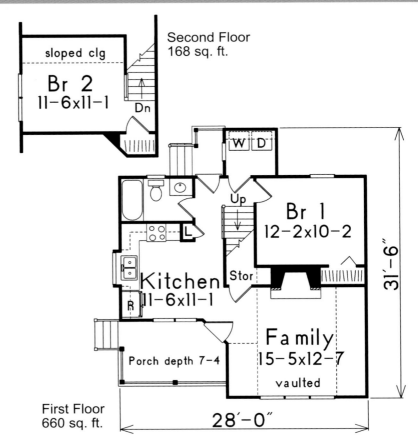

Second Floor
168 sq. ft.

sloped clg

Br 2
11-6x11-1

Dn

W D

Up

Br 1
12-2x10-2

Stor

31'-6"

Kitchen
11-6x11-1

R

L

Family
15-5x12-7

vaulted

Porch depth 7-4

First Floor
660 sq. ft.

28'-0"

**To order this plan, visit the Menards Building Materials Desk.**

**MENARDS**®

*Pondosa*

## Perfect Country Haven

1,232 total square feet of living area

### Special features

- Ideal porch for quiet quality evenings
- Great room opens to dining room for those large dinner gatherings
- Functional L-shaped kitchen includes broom cabinet
- Master bedroom contains a large walk-in closet and compartmented bath
- 3 bedrooms, 1 bath, optional 2-car garage
- Basement foundation, drawings also include crawl space and slab foundations

### Price Code A

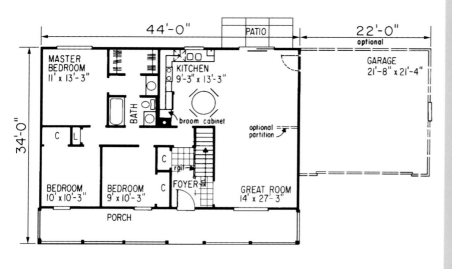

**MASTER BEDROOM** 11' x 13'-3"

**KITCHEN** 9'-3" x 13'-3"

broom cabinet

**BATH**

**GARAGE** 21'-8" x 21'-4"

optional partition

**BEDROOM** 10' x 10'-3"

**BEDROOM** 9' x 10'-3"

**FOYER**

**GREAT ROOM** 14' x 27'-3"

**PORCH**

44'-0"

34'-0"

**PATIO** optional

22'-0"

**MENARDS** ®

*Seneca*

## Rustic Design With Modern Features

1,000 total square feet of living area

### Special features

- Large mud room has a separate covered porch entrance
- Full-length covered front porch
- Bedrooms are on opposite sides of the home for privacy
- Vaulted ceiling creates an open and spacious feeling
- 2" x 6" exterior walls available, please order plan #M03-058D-0085
- 2 bedrooms, 1 bath
- Crawl space foundation

### Price Code AA

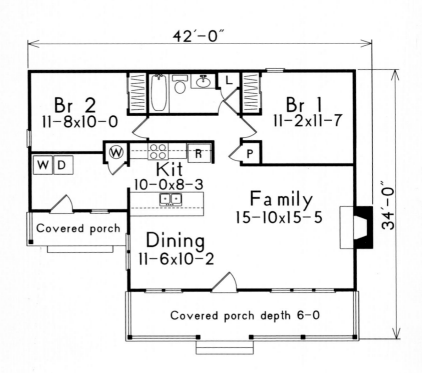

42'-0"

34'-0"

Br 2
11-8x10-0

Br 1
11-2x11-7

L

W D

Kit
10-0x8-3

R

P

W

Covered porch

Family
15-10x15-5

Dining
11-6x10-2

Covered porch depth 6-0

**To order this plan, visit the Menards Building Materials Desk.**

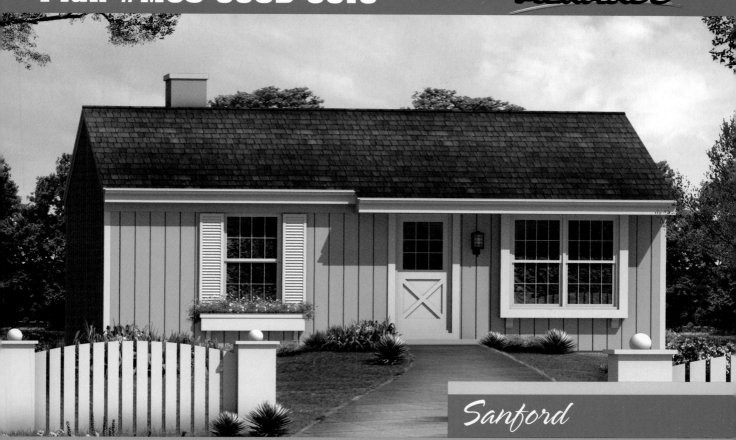

*Sanford*

## Functional Livability In A Small Ranch

768 total square feet of living area

### Special features

- Great room has an attractive box window for enjoying views
- Compact, yet efficient kitchen is open to the great room
- Six closets provide great storage for a compact plan
- Plans include optional third bedroom with an additional 288 square feet of living area
- 2 bedrooms, 1 bath
- Basement foundation, drawings also include crawl space and slab foundations

### Price Code AAA

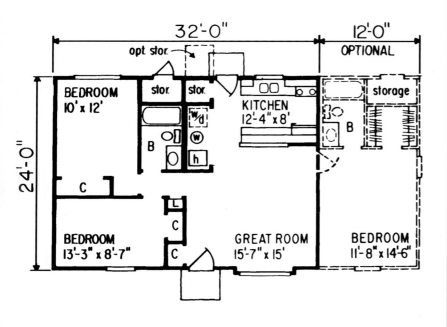

*Riverside*

## Large Loft Area Offers Endless Possibilities

1,426 total square feet of living area

### Special features

- Energy efficient home with 2" x 6" exterior walls
- Large front deck invites outdoor relaxation
- Expansive windows, skylights, vaulted ceiling and fireplace enhance the living and dining room combination
- Nook, adjacent to the living room, has a cozy window seat
- Kitchen is open to the living and dining rooms
- 1 bedroom, 1 bath
- Crawl space foundation

### Price Code A

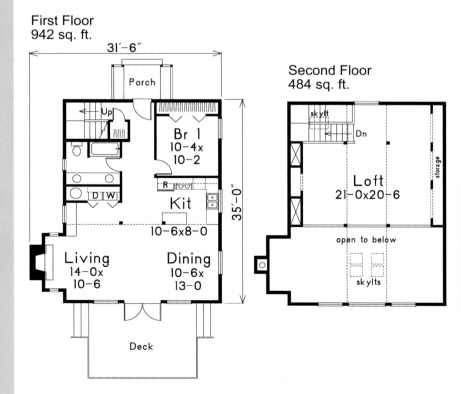

First Floor
942 sq. ft.

31'-6"

Porch

Up

Br 1
10-4x
10-2

35'-0"

Kit
10-6x8-0

Living
14-0x
10-6

Dining
10-6x
13-0

Deck

Second Floor
484 sq. ft.

skylt

Dn

Loft
21-0x20-6

storage

open to below

skylts

**To order this plan, visit the Menards Building Materials Desk.**

**MENARDS**®

If you clean brushes as soon as you're done painting for the day, the job will be a lot easier. Use warm, soapy water for water-based paints; for other coatings, use the solvent specified on the can. A brush is clean when the water or solvent runs clear, usually after 4 rinses. Don't leave the brush to soak because that can distort the bristles. Spin out excess cleaner, comb the bristles to straighten, and then lay the brush flat on a cloth to dry. Store it in a piece of folded newspaper to preserve its shape.

*Welton Park*

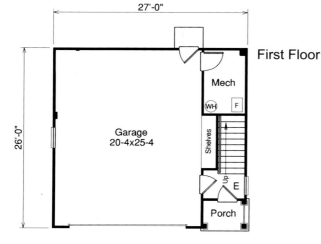

Second Floor
615 sq. ft.

Bedroom
12-0x11-0

Living Rm
14-0x13-0

Kitchen
6-4x11-0

First Floor

27'-0"

26'-0"

Garage
20-4x25-4

Mech

Shelves

Porch

## Apartment Garage With Lots Of Space

615 total square feet of living area

### Special features

- The handsome exterior includes a front porch and upper gabled box windows
- The first floor features an oversized two-car garage with built-in storage shelves and a large mechanical room
- A large living room with fireplace, entertainment alcove and kitchen open to an eating area are just a few of the many features of the second floor
- 1 bedroom, 1 bath, 2-car garage
- Slab foundation

### Price Code AAA

**To order this plan, visit the Menards Building Materials Desk.**

**MENARDS**®

*Grandale*

## Efficient Berm Home

1,643 total square feet of living area

### Special features

- Energy efficient home with 2" x 6" exterior walls
- The kitchen, living and dining rooms all combine for a spacious living area in this stylish, economical design
- An office, laundry room and half bath add conveniences for family living
- The massive master bedroom enjoys a deluxe bath with whirlpool tub and two walk-in closets
- 3 bedrooms, 2 1/2 baths, 1-car garage
- Slab foundation

### Price Code B

**To order this plan, visit the Menards Building Materials Desk.**

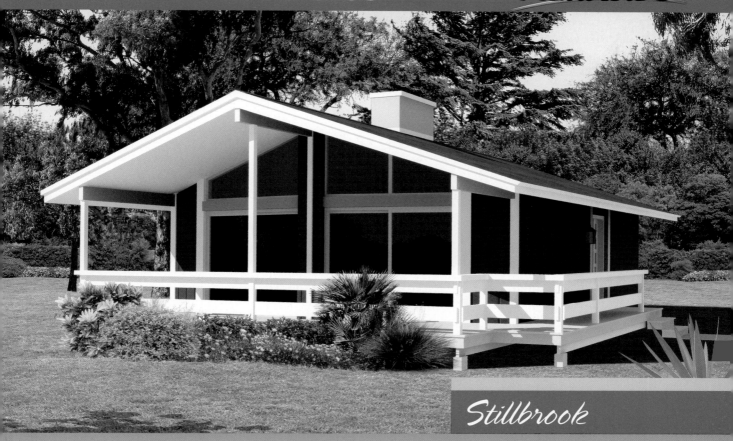

*Stillbrook*

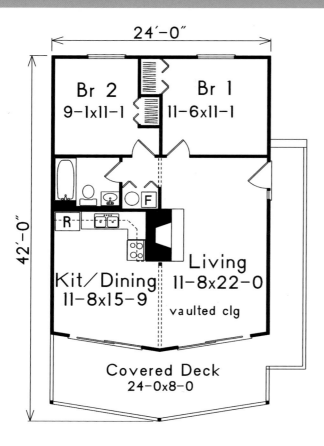

## Riverside Views From Covered Deck

792 total square feet of living area

### Special features

- Attractive exterior features wood posts and beams, wrap-around deck with railing and glass sliding doors with transoms
- Kitchen, living and dining areas enjoy sloped ceilings, a cozy fireplace and views over the deck
- Two bedrooms share a bath just off the hall
- 2 bedrooms, 1 bath
- Crawl space foundation, drawings also include slab foundation

### Price Code AAA

**To order this plan, visit the Menards Building Materials Desk.**

**MENARDS**®

*Darwin*

## Classic Ranch, Pleasant Covered Front Porch

1,416 total square feet of living area

### Special features

- Excellent floor plan eases traffic
- Master bedroom features private bath
- Foyer opens to both a formal living room and an informal great room
- Great room has access to the outdoors through sliding doors
- 3 bedrooms, 2 baths, 2-car garage
- Crawl space foundation, drawings also include basement foundation

### Price Code A

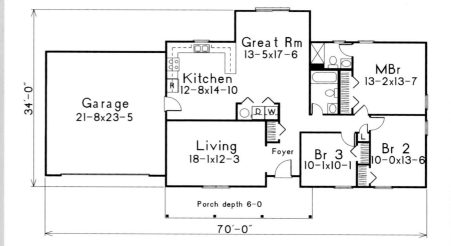

Great Rm
13-5x17-6

Kitchen
12-8x14-10

MBr
13-2x13-7

R

Garage
21-8x23-5

D W

Living
18-1x12-3

Foyer

Br 3
10-1x10-1

Br 2
10-0x13-6

34'-0"

Porch depth 6-0

70'-0"

**To order this plan, visit the Menards Building Materials Desk.**

*Riverview*

## Cozy Retreat For Weekends

480 total square feet of living area

### Special features

■ Inviting wrap-around porch and rear covered patio are perfect for summer evenings
■ Living room features a fireplace, separate entry foyer with coat closet and sliding doors to rear patio
■ The compact but complete kitchen includes a dining area with bay window and window at sink for patio views
■ 1 bedroom, 1 bath, 1-car garage
■ Slab foundation

### Price Code AAA

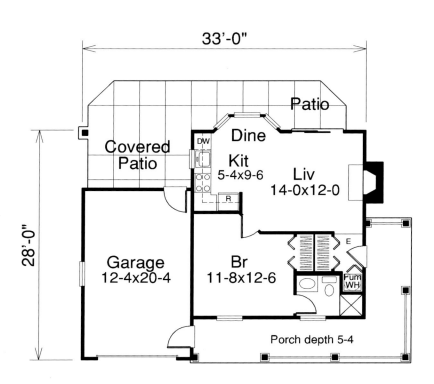

33'-0"

28'-0"

Patio

Covered Patio

Dine

Kit
5-4x9-6

Liv
14-0x12-0

Garage
12-4x20-4

Br
11-8x12-6

DW

R

Furn
WH

E

Porch depth 5-4

**To order this plan, visit the Menards Building Materials Desk.**

*Lena*

## Dramatic Sloping Ceiling In Living Room

1,432 total square feet of living area

### Special features

- Energy efficient home with 2" x 6" exterior walls
- Enter the two-story foyer from the covered porch or garage
- Living room has a square bay window with seat, glazed end wall with floor-to-ceiling windows and access to the deck
- Kitchen/dining room also opens to the deck for added convenience
- 3 bedrooms, 2 baths, 1-car garage
- Basement foundation, drawings also include slab foundation

**Price Code B**

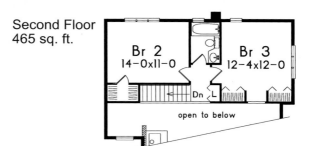

Second Floor
465 sq. ft.

Br 2
14-0x11-0

Br 3
12-4x12-0

Dn

open to below

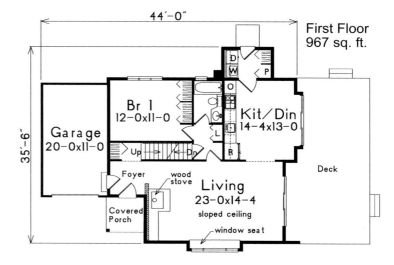

44'-0"

First Floor
967 sq. ft.

35'-6"

Garage
20-0x11-0

Br 1
12-0x11-0

Kit/Din
14-4x13-0

Up

Dn

Foyer

wood stove

Living
23-0x14-4
sloped ceiling

Covered Porch

window seat

Deck

**To order this plan, visit the Menards Building Materials Desk.**

*Timberhill*

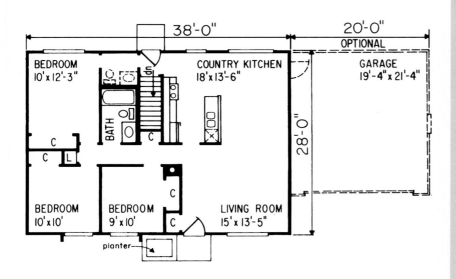

## Energy Efficient Design With Plenty Of Extras

1,064 total square feet of living area

### Special features

- Well-designed country kitchen
- Living room and kitchen unite to provide a central living area
- Lots of closet space throughout is perfect for ski storage or other sporting gear
- Unique built-in planter adds appeal to the front exterior
- 3 bedrooms, 1 1/2 baths, optional 2-car garage
- Basement foundation, drawings also include crawl space and slab foundations

**Price Code AA**

## Woodhaven

## Cozy Vacation Home

809 total square feet of living area

### Special features

- This attractive earth berm home is perfectly designed for a vacation retreat
- Nestled in a hillside with only one exposed exterior wall, this home offers efficiency, protection and affordability
- A large porch creates an ideal space for lazy afternoons and quiet evenings
- All rooms are very spacious and three closets plus the laundry room provide abundant storage
- 1 bedroom, 1 bath
- Slab foundation

### Price Code AAA

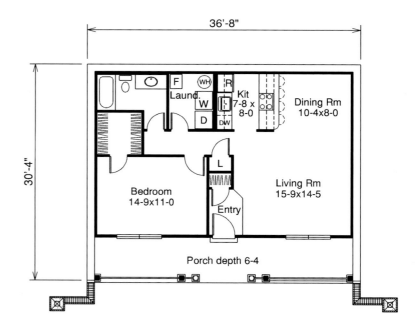

**To order this plan, visit the Menards Building Materials Desk.**

*Garland*

## Cozy And Functional Design

1,285 total square feet of living area

### Special features

- Dining nook creates a warm feeling with sunny box-bay window
- Second floor loft is perfect for a recreation space or office hideaway
- Bedrooms include walk-in closets allowing extra storage space
- Kitchen, dining and living areas combine making a perfect gathering place
- 2 bedrooms, 1 bath
- Crawl space foundation

### Price Code A

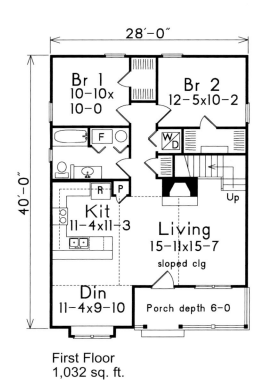

28'-0"

40'-0"

Br 1
10-10x
10-0

Br 2
12-5x10-2

F

W/D

R P

Kit
11-4x11-3

Up

Living
15-11x15-7
sloped clg

Din
11-4x9-10

Porch depth 6-0

**First Floor**
1,032 sq. ft.

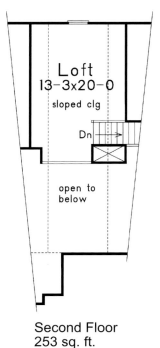

Loft
13-3x20-0
sloped clg

Dn

open to below

**Second Floor**
253 sq. ft.

## Birchmill

# Large Windows Brighten Home Inside And Out

1,260 total square feet of living area

### Special features

- Living area features an enormous stone fireplace and sliding glass doors for accessing the deck
- Kitchen/dining area is organized with lots of cabinet and counterspace
- Second bedroom is vaulted and has closet space along one entire wall
- 3 bedrooms, 1 bath
- Crawl space foundation

### Price Code A

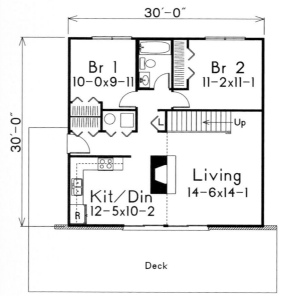

**First Floor**
900 sq. ft.

30'-0"

30'-0"

Br 1
10-0x9-11

Br 2
11-2x11-1

Kit/Din
12-5x10-2

Living
14-6x14-1

Up

Deck

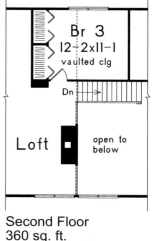

**Second Floor**
360 sq. ft.

Br 3
12-2x11-1
vaulted clg

Loft

open to below

Dn

76

Trees are a huge influence on a landscape so take time to locate them properly. Be careful when planting near a house - a tree that could spread 40 feet wide should be at least 20 feet from the house. Avoid planting where the tree will overhang your house, block a door, or obstruct a desirable view from inside. Plant where roots have ample room to grow. Don't plant a tree beneath power lines if it will grow to be 25 feet tall or more. Don't plant above underground utility lines. For help locating electric, cable, phone and water lines on your property, contact each of your utility companies directly.

*Oakhill*

## Two-Story Home Is A Perfect Fit For A Small Lot

858 total square feet of living area

### Special features

- Stackable washer/dryer is located in the kitchen
- Large covered porch graces this exterior
- Both bedrooms have walk-in closets
- 2 bedrooms, 1 bath
- Crawl space foundation

### Price Code AAA

**20'-0"**

**21'-0"**

Up

Din/Kit
15-8x8-6

W/D    R

Living
15-8x11-8

F

Porch depth 6-0

First Floor
420 sq. ft.

Br 2
10-4x9-8

Dn

Br 1
11-8x10-6

Second Floor
438 sq. ft.

**To order this plan, visit the Menards Building Materials Desk.**

*Haviland*

## 2-Car Garage Apartment

973 total square feet of living area

### Special features

- Side entry garage creates a garage apartment with the look of a two-story home
- Sunny breakfast room is positioned between the kitchen and the family room for convenience
- Both bedrooms are generously sized
- 2 bedrooms, 1 bath, 2-car side entry garage with storage
- Basement foundation

### Price Code AAA

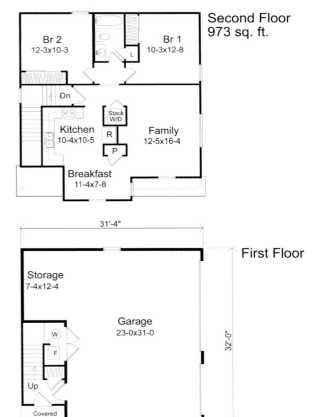

Second Floor
973 sq. ft.

Br 2
12-3x10-3

Br 1
10-3x12-8

L

Dn

Kitchen
10-4x10-5

Stack W/D

R

Family
12-5x16-4

P

Breakfast
11-4x7-8

31'-4"

First Floor

Storage
7-4x12-4

Garage
23-0x31-0

32'-0"

W

F

Up

Covered Porch

78

**To order this plan, visit the Menards Building Materials Desk.**

*Laketon*

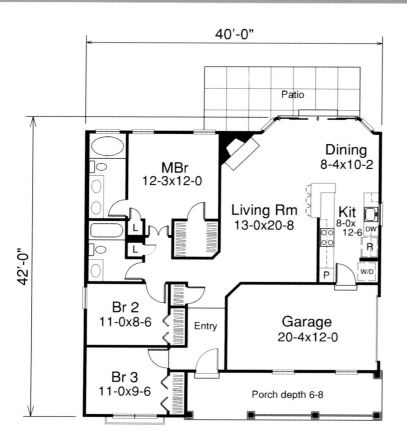

**40'-0"**

**42'-0"**

Patio

MBr
12-3x12-0

Living Rm
13-0x20-8

Dining
8-4x10-2

Kit
8-0x
12-6

DW

R

P

W/D

Br 2
11-0x8-6

Entry

Garage
20-4x12-0

Br 3
11-0x9-6

Porch depth 6-8

## Affordable Simplicity

1,196 total square feet of living area

### Special features

- Home includes an extra-deep porch for evening relaxation
- The large living room enjoys a corner fireplace, dining area featuring a wide bay window with sliding doors to the rear patio, and a snack bar open to the kitchen
- The master bedroom has a nice walk-in closet, its own linen closet and a roomy bath with a double-bowl vanity and garden tub
- 3 bedrooms, 2 baths, 1-car side entry garage
- Crawl space foundation, drawings also include slab foundation

### Price Code AA

# Plan #M03-007D-0173

Oakford

## Two-Story With A One-Story Disguise

2,121 total square feet of living area

### Special features

- The spacious great room includes a corner fireplace, dining area with bay window and glass sliding doors to the rear patio
- A huge center island with seating for six, built-in pantry and 26' of counterspace are just a few amenities of the awesome kitchen
- Three generously sized bedrooms, two baths and many walk-in closets comprise the second floor
- 4 bedrooms, 3 1/2 baths, 2-car garage
- Basement foundation, drawings also include slab and crawl space foundations

### Price Code C

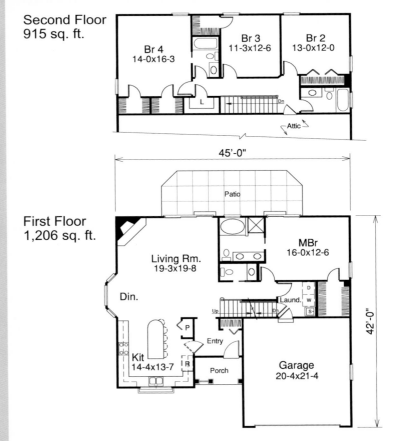

Second Floor
915 sq. ft.

Br 4
14-0x16-3

Br 3
11-3x12-6

Br 2
13-0x12-0

L

Dn

Attic

45'-0"

First Floor
1,206 sq. ft.

Patio

Living Rm.
19-3x19-8

MBr
16-0x12-6

Din.

Laund.

D
W
S

Up

42'-0"

P

Kit
14-4x13-7

R

Entry

Porch

Garage
20-4x21-4

**To order this plan, visit the Menards Building Materials Desk.**

*Barstow*

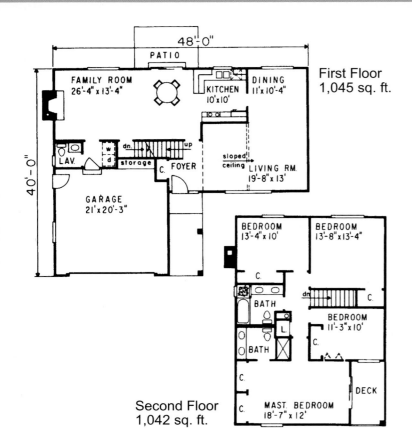

First Floor
1,045 sq. ft.

Second Floor
1,042 sq. ft.

## Contemporary Classic With Covered Deck

2,087 total square feet of living area

### Special features

- Family room with breakfast area offers outstanding size
- Plan includes a convenient half bath and first floor laundry
- Master bedroom enjoys two closets and access to a covered deck
- 4 bedrooms, 2 1/2 baths, 2-car garage
- Basement foundation, drawings also include crawl space and slab foundations

### Price Code C

**To order this plan, visit the Menards Building Materials Desk.**

*Woodhall*

## Gabled Front Porch Adds Charm And Value

1,443 total square feet of living area

### Special features

- Raised foyer and a cathedral ceiling in the living room add character to the interior
- Impressive tall-wall fireplace between the living and dining rooms
- Open U-shaped kitchen features a cheerful breakfast bay
- Angular side deck accentuates patio and garden
- First floor master bedroom has a walk-in closet and a corner window
- 3 bedrooms, 2 baths, 2-car garage
- Basement foundation

### Price Code A

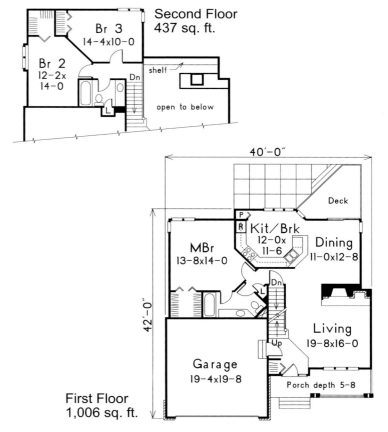

Second Floor
437 sq. ft.

Br 3
14-4x10-0

Br 2
12-2x
14-0

Dn

shelf

open to below

40'-0"

Deck

Kit/Brk
12-0x
11-6

MBr
13-8x14-0

Dining
11-0x12-8

42'-0"

Dn

Up

Living
19-8x16-0

Garage
19-4x19-8

Porch depth 5-8

First Floor
1,006 sq. ft.

**To order this plan, visit the Menards Building Materials Desk.**

*Birkhill*

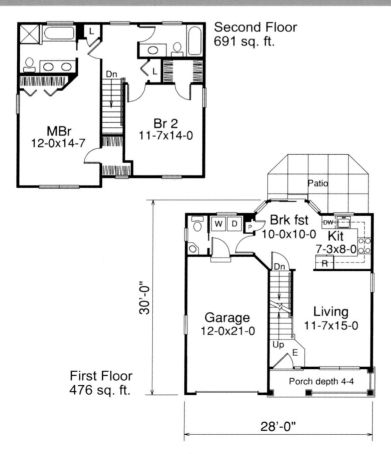

Second Floor
691 sq. ft.

MBr
12-0x14-7

Br 2
11-7x14-0

Dn

L

L

Patio

Brk fst
10-0x10-0

Kit
7-3x8-0

W  D  P

DW

R

Dn

Garage
12-0x21-0

Living
11-7x15-0

Up

E

30'-0"

First Floor
476 sq. ft.

Porch depth 4-4

28'-0"

## Compact Two-Story For A Small Site

1,167 total square feet of living area

### Special features

- Attractive exterior is enhanced with multiple gables
- Sizable living room features a separate entry foyer and view to front porch
- Functional kitchen has a breakfast room with bay window, built-in pantry and laundry room with half bath
- The master bedroom offers three closets and a luxury bath
- 2 bedrooms, 2 1/2 baths, 1-car garage
- Basement foundation

### Price Code AA

**MENARDS**®

*Skyliner*

## A Home Designed For Hillside Views

**1,806 total square feet of living area**

### Special features

- Wrap-around deck, great for entertaining, enhances appearance
- Side entry foyer accesses two rear bedrooms, hall bath and living and dining area
- L-shaped kitchen is open to dining areas
- Lots of living area is provided on the lower level, including a spacious family room with a fireplace and sliding doors to the patio under the deck
- 3 bedrooms, 2 baths
- Walk-out basement foundation

**Price Code C**

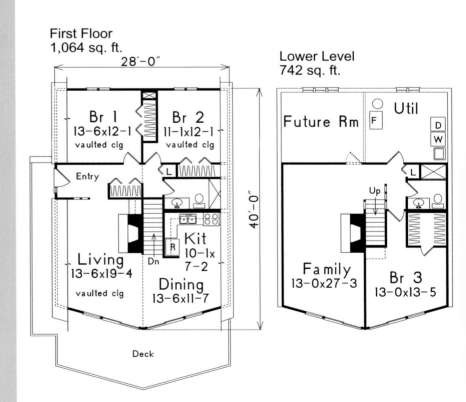

First Floor
1,064 sq. ft.

28'-0"

Br 1
13-6x12-1
vaulted clg

Br 2
11-1x12-1
vaulted clg

Entry

40'-0"

Kit
10-1x
7-2

Living
13-6x19-4
vaulted clg

Dn

Dining
13-6x11-7

Deck

Lower Level
742 sq. ft.

Future Rm

Util

F

D

W

Up

Family
13-0x27-3

Br 3
13-0x13-5

**To order this plan, visit the Menards Building Materials Desk.**

*Prairie View*

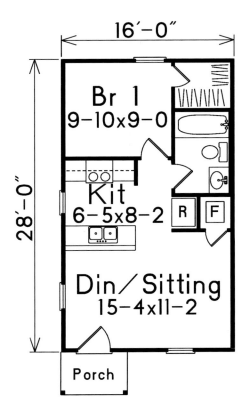

16'-0"

Br 1
9-10x9-0

28'-0"

Kit
6-5x8-2

R  F

Din/Sitting
15-4x11-2

Porch

## Irresistible Retreat

448 total square feet of living area

### Special features
- Bedroom features a large walk-in closet ideal for storage
- Combined dining/sitting area is ideal for relaxing
- Galley-style kitchen is compact and efficient
- Covered porch adds to front facade
- 1 bedroom, 1 bath
- Slab foundation

### Price Code AAA

**To order this plan, visit the Menards Building Materials Desk.**

# Plan #M03-022D-0021

*Villawood*

## Breakfast Bay Area Opens To Deck

1,020 total square feet of living area

### Special features

- Kitchen features open stairs, pass-through to great room, pantry and deck access
- Master bedroom features private entrance to bath, large walk-in closet and sliding doors to deck
- Informal entrance into home through the garage
- Great room has a vaulted ceiling and fireplace
- 2 bedrooms, 1 bath, 2-car garage
- Basement foundation

### Price Code AA

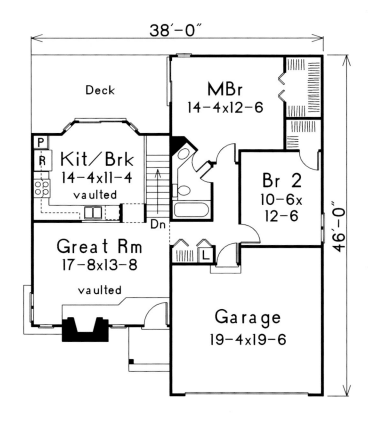

38'-0"

46'-0"

Deck

MBr
14-4x12-6

Kit/Brk
14-4x11-4
vaulted

P
R

Br 2
10-6x
12-6

Dn

Great Rm
17-8x13-8
vaulted

L

Garage
19-4x19-6

**To order this plan, visit the Menards Building Materials Desk.**

*Park House*

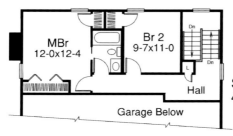

MBr
12-0x12-4

Br 2
9-7x11-0

Dn

Hall

L

Dn

**Second Floor
492 sq. ft.**

Garage Below

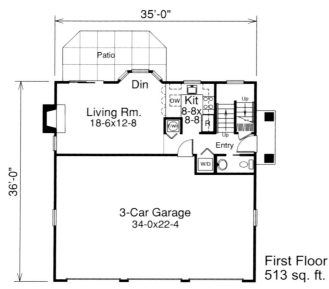

35'-0"

Patio

Din

Living Rm.
18-6x12-8

Kit
8-8x
8-8

DW

Up

Up

R

Entry

W/D

36'-0"

3-Car Garage
34-0x22-4

**First Floor
513 sq. ft.**

## Three-Car Garage With Rear Apartment

1,005 total square feet of living area

### Special features

- Two-story apartment is disguised with a one-story facade featuring triple garage doors and a roof dormer
- Side porch leads to an entry hall which accesses the living room, U-shaped kitchen, powder room and stairs to second floor
- The large living room has a fireplace, sliding doors to the rear patio, dining area with bay window and opens to the kitchen with breakfast bar
- The second floor is comprised of two bedrooms and a bath
- 2 bedrooms, 1 1/2 baths, 3-car garage
- Slab foundation

### Price Code AA

**To order this plan, visit the Menards Building Materials Desk.**

*Cedarville*

## Simply Country

1,668 total square feet of living area

### Special features

- Simple, but attractively styled ranch home is perfect for a narrow lot
- Front entry porch flows into the foyer which connects to the living room
- Garage entrance to home leads to the kitchen through the mud room/laundry area
- U-shaped kitchen opens to the dining area and family room
- Three bedrooms are situated at the rear of the home with two full baths
- Master bedroom has a walk-in closet
- 3 bedrooms, 2 baths, 2-car garage
- Partial basement/crawl space foundation, drawings also include crawl space and slab foundations

### Price Code B

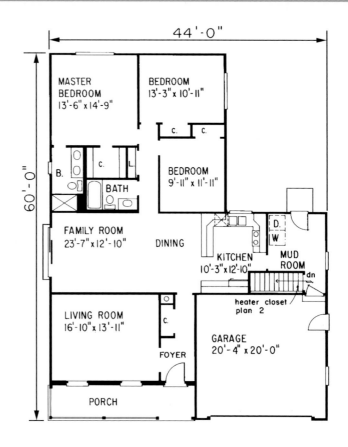

**To order this plan, visit the Menards Building Materials Desk.**

*Woodbriar*

## Vacation Cabin

480 total square feet of living area

### Special features

- Energy efficient home with 2" x 6" exterior walls
- A wide, covered porch greets guests and offers a grand outdoor living space
- A fireplace warms the cozy sitting area that is adjacent to the dining room
- The bedroom enjoys a walk-in closet for easy organization
- 1 bedroom, 1 bath
- Basement foundation

### Price Code AAA

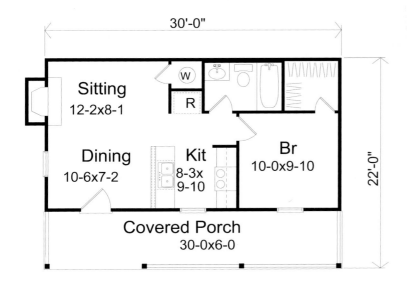

30'-0"

Sitting
12-2x8-1

W
R

Dining
10-6x7-2

Kit
8-3x
9-10

Br
10-0x9-10

22'-0"

Covered Porch
30-0x6-0

**To order this plan, visit the Menards Building Materials Desk.**

*Dunhill*

# Four-Car Apartment Garage With Shop

831 total square feet of living area

## Special features

- Attractive single-story look with an elegant gabled porch
- Shop room includes built-in cabinets, a half bath, both single-car and two-car garages and accesses the large front porch
- The second floor apartment features a living room with rear balcony, efficient kitchen with snack bar and spacious bedroom with hall bath
- 1 bedroom, 1 1/2 baths, 4-car rear entry garage
- Slab foundation

### Price Code AAA

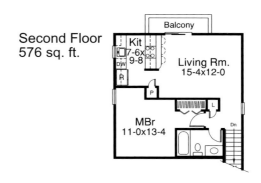

Second Floor
576 sq. ft.

Balcony

Kit
7-6x
9-8

Living Rm.
15-4x12-0

MBr
11-0x13-4

Dn

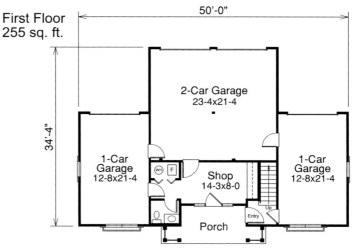

First Floor
255 sq. ft.

50'-0"

34'-4"

2-Car Garage
23-4x21-4

1-Car Garage
12-8x21-4

Shop
14-3x8-0

1-Car Garage
12-8x21-4

Entry

Porch

**To order this plan, visit the Menards Building Materials Desk.**

# Plan #M03-057D-0021

**MENARDS**®

*Copeland*

## First Floor / Second Floor Plans

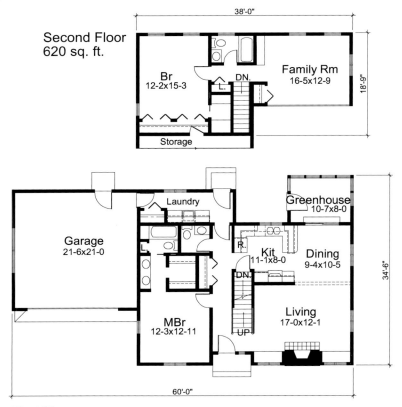

**Second Floor**
620 sq. ft.

- 38'-0"
- 18'-9"
- Br 12-2x15-3
- DN.
- L.
- Family Rm 16-5x12-9
- Storage

**First Floor**
1,079 sq. ft.

- Laundry
- Garage 21-6x21-0
- L.
- R.
- Greenhouse 10-7x8-0
- Kit 11-1x8-0
- Dining 9-4x10-5
- DN.
- MBr 12-3x12-11
- UP
- Living 17-0x12-1
- 34'-6"
- 60'-0"

## Contemporary Design

2,615 total square feet of living area

### Special features

- Energy efficient home with 2" x 6" exterior walls
- Both formal and informal living spaces are graced with stylish fireplaces
- Enjoy the large deck and sunroom located off the dining room
- 2 bedrooms, 2 1/2 baths, 2-car garage
- Basement foundation

### Price Code E

**To order this plan, visit the Menards Building Materials Desk.**

*Alpine*

## Apartment Garage With Imagination

654 total square feet of living area

### Special features

- Two-story vaulted entry has a balcony overlook and large windows to welcome the sun
- Vaulted living room is open to a pass-through kitchen and breakfast bar with an overhead plant shelf and features sliding glass doors to an outdoor balcony
- The bedroom with vaulted ceiling offers a private bath and walk-in closet
- 1 bedroom, 1 bath, 2-car garage
- Slab foundation

### Price Code AAA

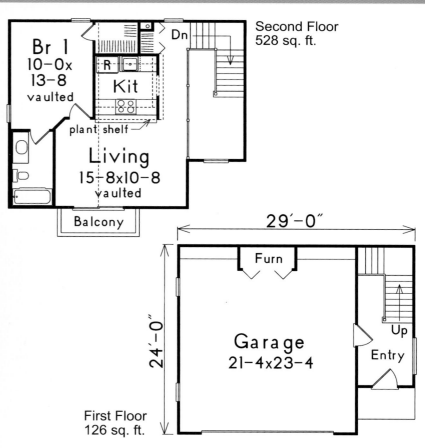

Second Floor
528 sq. ft.

Br 1
10-0x
13-8
vaulted

Kit

R

Dn

plant shelf

Living
15-8x10-8
vaulted

Balcony

First Floor
126 sq. ft.

29'-0"

24'-0"

Furn

Garage
21-4x23-4

Up

Entry

**To order this plan, visit the Menards Building Materials Desk.**

# Plan #M03-008D-0150

Fireplaces are consistently rated as one of the top amenities desired by home-owners. In fact, fireplaces have one of the highest investment returns of any addition to your home. Here are a few tips to keep safe when using your beautiful fireplace: When you light the fire keep the flue fully open, for maximum airflow to feed the flames. Once it's roaring, close the flue to the point where the chimney starts smoking, then open it just a tad for optimal heat. To keep airflow constant and avoid carbon monoxide buildup, open the window closest to the fire by a half-inch. And make sure to keep a fire extinguisher handy, because even a "dead" fire can suddenly emit random, carpet-igniting sparks.

## Inglewood

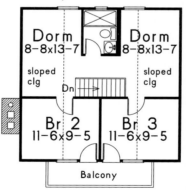

**Second Floor**
528 sq. ft.

- Dorm 8-8x13-7
- sloped clg
- Dorm 8-8x13-7
- sloped clg
- Dn
- Br 2 11-6x9-5
- Br 3 11-6x9-5
- Balcony

**First Floor**
576 sq. ft.

- 26'-8"
- Br 1 9-4x10-3
- Kit 8-1x 9-1
- R
- Dn Up
- Living/Dining 23-4x12-9
- 24'-0"
- Deck

**Lower Level**
576 sq. ft.

- Workshop 13-4x9-7
- D W
- F
- Up
- Ski Lounge 14-1x12-9
- Wet Hall

## Ski Chalet With Style

1,680 total square feet of living area

### Special features

- Highly functional lower level includes a wet hall with storage, laundry area, workshop and cozy ski lounge with an enormous fireplace
- First floor is warmed by a large fireplace in the living/dining area which features a spacious wrap-around deck
- Lots of sleeping space for guests or a large family
- 5 bedrooms, 2 1/2 baths
- Walk-out basement foundation

### Price Code B

**To order this plan, visit the Menards Building Materials Desk.**

**MENARDS**®

*Argyle*

## Small Ranch With Three-Car Garage And Covered Deck

1,348 total square feet of living area

### Special features

- Ideal retirement home or lakeside retreat with a country flavor
- The living room has a stone corner fireplace and carefully planned shelving for a flat panel TV and components
- A luxury bath, huge walk-in closet and covered deck adjoin the master bedroom
- The lower level is comprised of a guest bedroom, hall bath and garage with space for two cars and a boat
- 2 bedrooms, 2 1/2 baths, 3-car rear entry drive under garage
- Walk-out basement foundation

### Price Code A

First Floor 1,008 sq. ft.

45'-0"

Covered Deck

Living Rm 14-3x16-9

Dining 9-4x9-4

24'-0"

MBr 12-0x15-4

Kit 9-4x 14-0

Entry

shelves

Dn

Porch depth 5-0

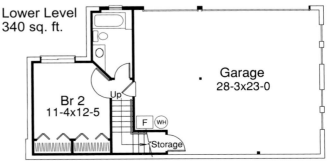

Lower Level 340 sq. ft.

Br 2 11-4x12-5

Up

Garage 28-3x23-0

Storage

**To order this plan, visit the Menards Building Materials Desk.**

*Hickory Lake*

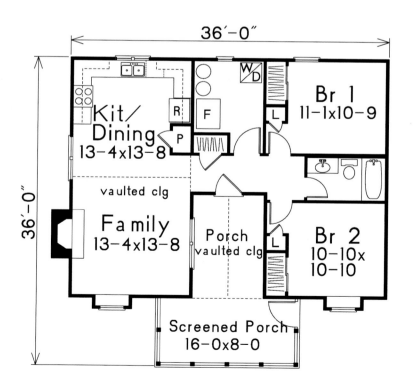

## Excellent For Weekend Entertaining

924 total square feet of living area

### Special features

- Box-bay window seats brighten the interior while enhancing the front facade
- Spacious kitchen with lots of cabinet space and a large pantry
- T-shaped covered porch is screened for added enjoyment
- Plenty of closet space throughout with linen closets in both bedrooms
- 2 bedrooms, 1 bath
- Slab foundation

### Price Code AA

**To order this plan, visit the Menards Building Materials Desk.**

*Darbytown*

## English Cottage With Modern Amenities

1,816 total square feet of living area

### Special features

- The living room features a two-way fireplace with nearby window seat
- Wrap-around dining room windows create a sunroom appearance
- Master bedroom has abundant closet and storage space
- Rear dormers, closets and desk areas create an interesting and functional second floor
- 3 bedrooms, 2 1/2 baths, 2-car detached garage
- Slab foundation, drawings also include crawl space foundation

**Price Code C**

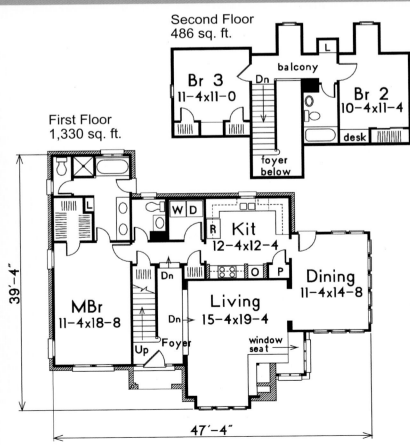

Second Floor
486 sq. ft.

Br 3
11-4x11-0

balcony

Dn

L

Br 2
10-4x11-4

desk

foyer below

First Floor
1,330 sq. ft.

39'-4"

47'-4"

MBr
11-4x18-8

Dn

W D

R

Kit
12-4x12-4

Dn

O P

Dining
11-4x14-8

Living
15-4x19-4

Foyer

Up

Dn

window seat

**To order this plan, visit the Menards Building Materials Desk.**

*Winterfarm*

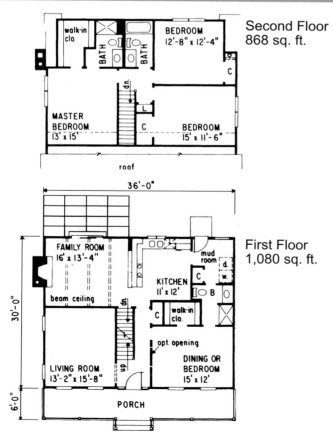

Second Floor
868 sq. ft.

First Floor
1,080 sq. ft.

## Well-Designed Home Makes Great Use Of Space

1,948 total square feet of living area

### Special features

■ Family room offers warmth with an oversized fireplace and rustic beamed ceiling
■ Fully-appointed kitchen extends into the family room
■ Practical mud room is adjacent to the kitchen
■ 3 bedrooms, 2 1/2 baths
■ Basement foundation, drawings also include crawl space foundation

## Price Code C

**To order this plan, visit the Menards Building Materials Desk.**

# Plan #M03-007D-0138

*Brookstone*

## A Lasting First Impression

2,167 total square feet of living area

### Special features

- Multi-gables with window shutters and plant boxes combined with stone veneer, create an elegant country facade
- L-shaped kitchen has work island snack bar open to bayed breakfast room and large family room to provide a 40' vista
- Entry and breakfast room access second floor via T-stair
- Vaulted master bedroom has a walk-in closet adjacent to luxury master bath
- 4 bedrooms, 2 1/2 baths, 2-car garage
- Basement foundation

## Price Code C

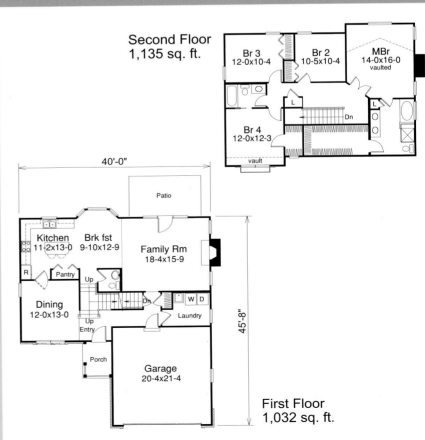

Second Floor
1,135 sq. ft.

Br 3
12-0x10-4

Br 2
10-5x10-4

MBr
14-0x16-0
vaulted

Br 4
12-0x12-3

vault

40'-0"

Patio

Kitchen
11-2x13-0

Brk fst
9-10x12-9

Family Rm
18-4x15-9

Pantry

Up

Dining
12-0x13-0

Up
Entry

Dn

W D

Laundry

Porch

Garage
20-4x21-4

45'-8"

First Floor
1,032 sq. ft.

**To order this plan, visit the Menards Building Materials Desk.**

**MENARDS**®

*Greentree*

## Second Floor
745 sq. ft.

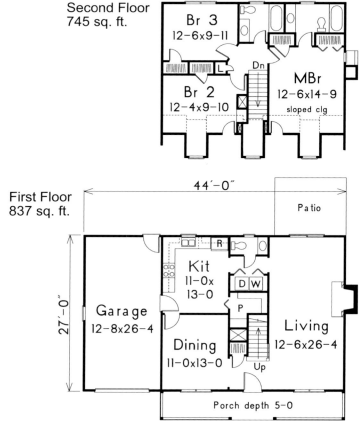

Br 3
12-6x9-11

Dn

Br 2
12-4x9-10

L

MBr
12-6x14-9
sloped clg

## First Floor
837 sq. ft.

44'-0"

Patio

27'-0"

Garage
12-8x26-4

Kit
11-0x
13-0

R

D W

P

Dining
11-0x13-0

Up

Living
12-6x26-4

Porch depth 5-0

# Trim Colonial For Practical Living

1,582 total square feet of living area

## Special features

- Conservative layout gives privacy to living and dining areas
- Large fireplace and windows enhance the living area
- Rear door in garage is convenient to the garden and kitchen
- Full front porch adds charm
- Dormers add light to the foyer and bedrooms
- 3 bedrooms, 2 1/2 baths, 1-car garage
- Slab foundation, drawings also include crawl space foundation

## Price Code B

**To order this plan, visit the Menards Building Materials Desk.**

*Summercreek*

## Master Bedroom Is Spacious And Private

1,160 total square feet of living area

### Special features

- Kitchen/dining area combines with the laundry area creating a functional and organized space
- Spacious vaulted living area has a large fireplace and is brightened by glass doors accessing the large deck
- Ascend to the second floor loft by spiral stairs and find a cozy hideaway
- Master bedroom is brightened by many windows and includes a private bath and double closets
- 1 bedroom, 1 bath
- Crawl space foundation

**Price Code AA**

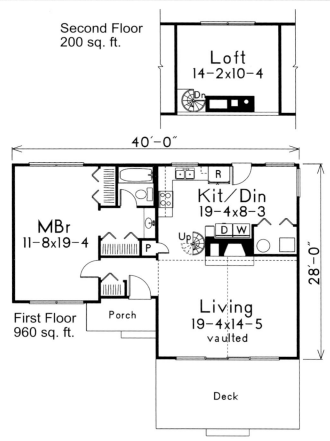

Second Floor
200 sq. ft.

Loft
14-2x10-4

40'-0"

MBr
11-8x19-4

Kit/Din
19-4x8-3

Living
19-4x14-5
vaulted

28'-0"

Porch

First Floor
960 sq. ft.

Deck

**To order this plan, visit the Menards Building Materials Desk.**

*Kaywood*

## Charming Home With Cozy Porches

1,107 total square feet of living area

### Special features

- L-shaped kitchen has serving bar overlooking the dining/living room
- Second floor bedrooms share a bath with linen closet
- Front porch opens into foyer with convenient coat closet
- 3 bedrooms, 2 baths
- Basement foundation

### Price Code AA

First Floor
682 sq. ft.

Porch depth 4-0

R

Kit
9-7x11-0

Br 1
11-3x11-7

Dining Living
13-5x18-3

Dn

Up

Porch depth
4-0

34'-0"

22'-0"

Second Floor
425 sq. ft.

Br 3
9-0x10-7

L

L

Dn

Br 2
9-0x10-0

**To order this plan, visit the Menards Building Materials Desk.**

## Ericson

# 2-Car Garage Apartment

868 total square feet of living area

### Special features

- Large windows brighten the adjoining dining and great rooms
- The efficient kitchen includes a snack bar counter connecting to the dining room
- A linen closet and utility room provide essential storage space
- 1 bedroom, 1 bath, 2-car garage
- Basement foundation

## Price Code AAA

Second Floor
868 sq. ft.

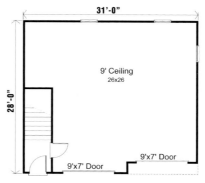

First Floor

**To order this plan, visit the Menards Building Materials Desk.**

**MENARDS®**

*Summerplace*

## Two Bedroom Cottage With Garage And Shop

801 total square feet of living area

### Special features

- A wrap-around porch, roof dormer and fancy stonework all contribute to a delightful and charming exterior
- The living room enjoys a separate entry, a stone fireplace, vaulted ceiling and lots of windows
- The well-equipped kitchen has a snack bar and dining area with bay which offers access to the rear patio
- An oversized two-car garage features a large vaulted room ideal for a shop, studio, hobby room or office with built-in cabinets and access to the porch
- 2 bedrooms, 1 bath, 2-car side entry garage
- Slab foundation

### Price Code AAA

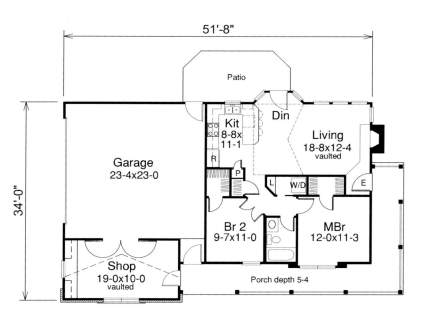

**To order this plan, visit the Menards Building Materials Desk.**

103

foundation

### Price Code C

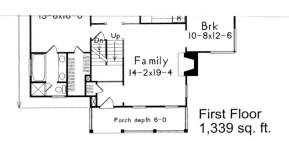

First Floor
1,339 sq. ft.

**To order this plan, visit the Menards Building Materials Desk.**

# Plan #M03-007D-0134

**MENARDS**®

*Foxmyer*

## Affordable Simplicity

1,310 total square feet of living area

### Special features

- The combination of brick quoins, roof dormers and an elegant porch creates a classic look
- Open-space floor plan has vaulted kitchen, living and dining rooms
- The master bedroom is vaulted and enjoys privacy from other bedrooms
- A spacious laundry room is convenient to the kitchen and master bedroom with access to an oversized garage
- 3 bedrooms, 2 baths, 2-car garage
- Basement foundation, drawings also include crawl space and slab foundations

### Price Code A

73'-0"

Patio
12-0x9-0

Br 2
11-4x9-6

Dining
11-0x13-0
vaulted

Kitchen
10-0x9-5
vaulted

Laund.

W
D

Garage
21-4x25-4

26'-0"

Br 3
11-4x10-1

Living Room
20-0x12-1
vaulted

MBr
11-6x15-7
vaulted

Porch depth 6-2

**To order this plan, visit the Menards Building Materials Desk.**

**MENARDS**®

*Pinecone*

## Corner Window Wall Dominates Design

784 total square feet of living area

### Special features

- Outdoor relaxation will be enjoyed with this home's huge wrap-around wood deck
- Upon entering the spacious living area, a cozy free-standing fireplace, sloped ceiling and corner window wall catch the eye
- Charming kitchen features pass-through peninsula to dining area
- 3 bedrooms, 1 bath
- Pier foundation

### Price Code AAA

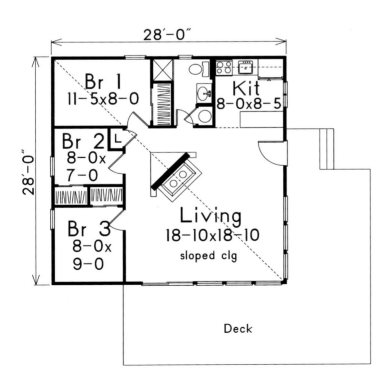

28'-0"

28'-0"

Br 1
11-5x8-0

Kit
8-0x8-5

Br 2
8-0x
7-0

Br 3
8-0x
9-0

Living
18-10x18-10
sloped clg

Deck

**To order this plan, visit the Menards Building Materials Desk.**

**MENARDS**®

*Barrett*

## Comfortable Vacation Retreat

1,073 total square feet of living area

### Special features

- Home includes a lovely covered front porch and a screened porch off the dining area
- Attractive box window brightens the kitchen
- Space for an efficiency washer and dryer is located conveniently between the bedrooms
- Family room is spotlighted by a fireplace with flanking bookshelves and spacious vaulted ceiling
- 2 bedrooms, 1 bath
- Crawl space foundation

### Price Code AA

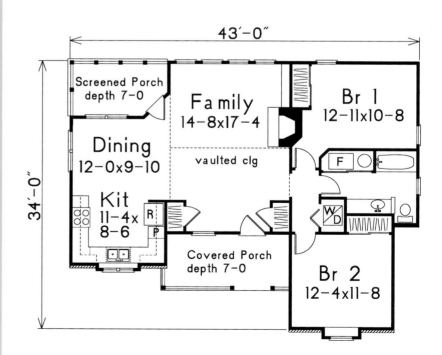

**To order this plan, visit the Menards Building Materials Desk.**

*Silverpine*

## Split Bedroom Cottage Home

1,202 total square feet of living area

### Special features

- All the necessary ingredients provided in a simple structure that's affordable to build
- The vaulted living room features a fireplace, dining area and access to the rear patio
- An angled snack bar is the highlight of this well-planned U-shaped kitchen
- 3 bedrooms, 2 baths, 2-car side entry garage
- Basement foundation, drawings also include slab and crawl space foundations

### Price Code A

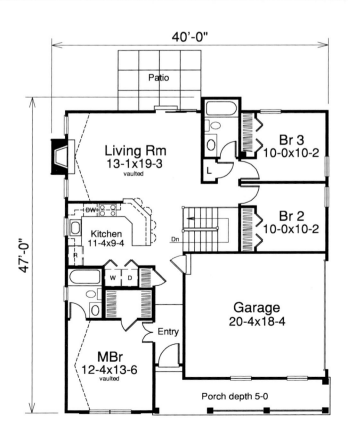

**To order this plan, visit the Menards Building Materials Desk.**

## Leisure Time

## Perfect Home For Escaping To The Outdoors

1,200 total square feet of living area

### Special features

- Enjoy lazy summer evenings on this magnificent porch
- Activity area has a fireplace and ascending stair from the cozy loft
- Kitchen features a built-in pantry
- Master bedroom enjoys a large bath, walk-in closet and cozy loft overlooking the room below
- 2 bedrooms, 2 baths
- Crawl space foundation

### Price Code A

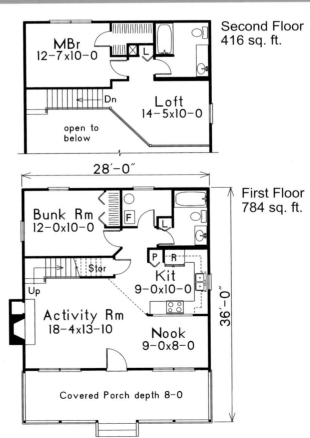

Second Floor
416 sq. ft.

MBr
12-7x10-0

L

Dn

Loft
14-5x10-0

open to below

28'-0"

First Floor
784 sq. ft.

Bunk Rm
12-0x10-0

F

L

Stor

P R

Kit
9-0x10-0

Up

Activity Rm
18-4x13-10

Nook
9-0x8-0

36'-0"

Covered Porch depth 8-0

**To order this plan, visit the Menards Building Materials Desk.**

*Springhill*

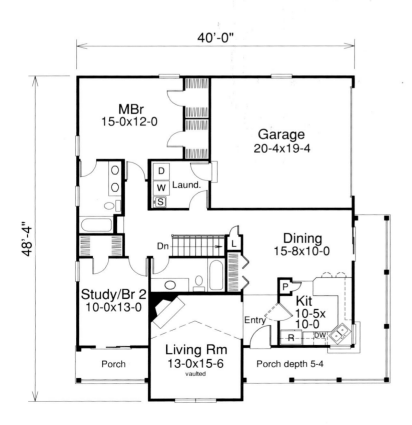

40'-0"

MBr
15-0x12-0

Garage
20-4x19-4

48'-4"

D
W  Laund.
S

Dn  L

Dining
15-8x10-0

Study/Br 2
10-0x13-0

P
Kit
10-5x
10-0

R  DW

Entry

Living Rm
13-0x15-6
vaulted

Porch

Porch depth 5-4

## Porches Enhance Small Retirement Or Starter Home

1,316 total square feet of living area

### Special features

- Porches are accessible from entry, dining room and bedroom #2
- The living room enjoys a vaulted ceiling, corner fireplace and twin windows with an arched transom above
- A kitchen is provided with corner windows, an outdoor plant shelf, a snack bar, a built-in pantry and opens to a large dining room
- Bedrooms are very roomy, feature walk-in closets and have easy access to oversized baths
- 2 bedrooms, 2 baths, 2-car side entry garage
- Basement foundation, drawings also include crawl space and slab foundations

**Price Code A**

*Summertree*

## Versatile Cottage Has Many Uses

1,131 total square feet of living area

### Special features

- Inviting porch and roof dormer create a charming exterior
- The spacious area on the first floor is perfect for a large shop, private studio, office or cottage great room and includes a fireplace, kitchenette and half bath
- Two bedrooms, a full bath and attic storage comprise the second floor which has its own private entrance and wide sunny hallway
- 2 bedrooms, 1 1/2 baths
- Slab foundation

### Price Code AA

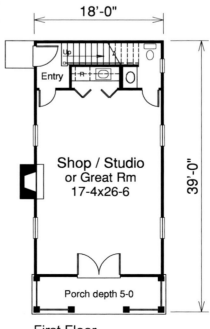

First Floor
612 sq. ft.

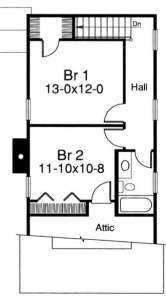

Second Floor
519 sq. ft.

**To order this plan, visit the Menards Building Materials Desk.**

*Spring Valley*

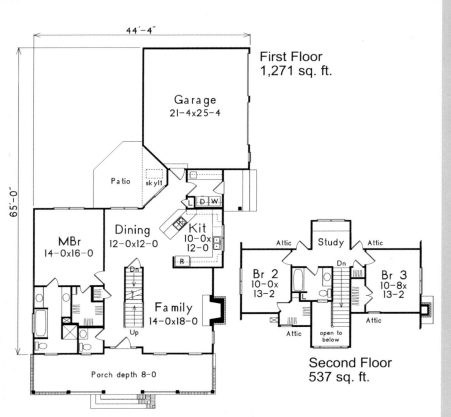

First Floor
1,271 sq. ft.

Garage
21-4x25-4

Patio

sk ylt

D W

MBr
14-0x16-0

Dining
12-0x12-0

Kit
10-0x
12-0

R

Dn

Family
14-0x18-0

Up

44'-4"

65'-0"

Porch depth 8-0

Attic  Study  Attic

Br 2
10-0x
13-2

Dn

Br 3
10-8x
13-2

Attic

Attic

open to
below

Second Floor
537 sq. ft.

## Covered Porch Highlights Home

1,808 total square feet of living area

### Special features

- Master bedroom has a walk-in closet, double vanities and a separate tub and shower
- Two second floor bedrooms share a study area and full bath
- Partially covered patio is complete with a skylight
- Side entrance opens to utility room with convenient counterspace and laundry sink
- 3 bedrooms, 2 1/2 baths, 2-car side entry garage
- Basement foundation

### Price Code C

*Brookview*

## Unique Yet Functional Design

1,316 total square feet of living area

### Special features

- Massive vaulted family/living room is accented with a fireplace and views to the outdoors through sliding glass doors
- Galley-style kitchen is centrally located
- Unique separate shower room near bath doubles as a convenient mud room
- 3 bedrooms, 1 bath
- Crawl space foundation

### Price Code A

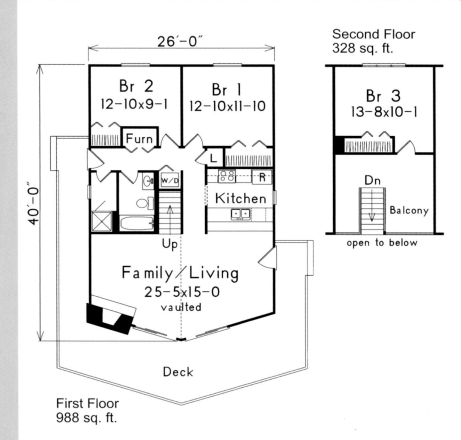

Second Floor
328 sq. ft.

Br 3
13-8x10-1

Dn

Balcony

open to below

26'-0"

40'-0"

Br 2
12-10x9-1

Br 1
12-10x11-10

Furn

W/D

L

R

Kitchen

Up

Family/Living
25-5x15-0
vaulted

Deck

First Floor
988 sq. ft.

**To order this plan, visit the Menards Building Materials Desk.**

**MENARDS**®

*St. Charles*

Second Floor
1,015 sq. ft.

Br 3
11-0x11-0

Br 2
9-6x10-0

Dn

Br 4
13-4x11-7

MBr
13-0x16-11

coffered clg.

37'-0"

Patio

Brk fst.
10-6x14-1

Kitchen
10-6x12-1

Great Room
13-4x21-6

Dn

R

P

D  W  S

Up

Dining
17-4x11-0

tray clg.

Entry

Porch depth 5-4

49'-8"

Garage
19-4x20-4

First Floor
1,031 sq. ft.

## Classy Two-Story Perfectly Suited For A Narrow Lot

2,046 total square feet of living area

### Special features

- Hipped roof and special brickwork provide nice curb appeal
- The kitchen and breakfast room offer island cabinetry, a walk-in pantry, wide bay window and easy access to a large dining room
- Cheery transom windows and fireplace are just two amenities of the huge great room
- The second floor has large secondary bedrooms and a spacious master bedroom with a double-door entry, double walk-in closets and a luxury bath with corner tub
- 4 bedrooms, 2 1/2 baths, 2-car garage
- Basement foundation

**Price Code C**

**To order this plan, visit the Menards Building Materials Desk.**

## Forestville

## Covered Porch Adds Charm To Entrance

1,655 total square feet of living area

### Special features

- Master bedroom features a 9' ceiling, walk-in closet and bath with dressing area
- Oversized family room includes a 10' ceiling and masonry see-through fireplace
- Island kitchen has convenient access to the laundry room
- Handy covered walkway from the garage leads to the kitchen and dining area
- 3 bedrooms, 2 baths, 2-car garage
- Crawl space foundation

### Price Code B

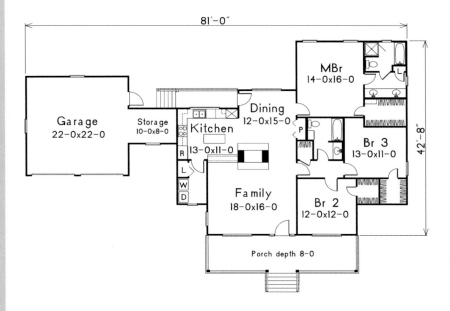

**To order this plan, visit the Menards Building Materials Desk.**

*Candlewick*

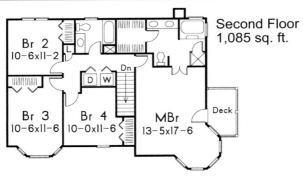

Second Floor
1,085 sq. ft.

Br 2
10-6x11-2

D W

Dn

Deck

Br 3
10-6x11-6

Br 4
10-0x11-6

MBr
13-5x17-6

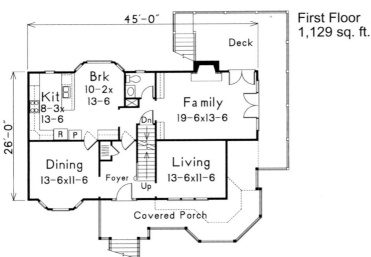

45'-0"

First Floor
1,129 sq. ft.

Deck

26'-0"

Brk
10-2x
13-6

Kit
8-3x
13-6

Family
19-6x13-6

Dn

R P

Dining
13-6x11-6

Foyer

Living
13-6x11-6

Up

Covered Porch

# Victorian Turret Provides Dramatic Focus

2,214 total square feet of living area

## Special features

- Victorian accents dominate facade
- Covered porches and decks fan out to connect front and rear entries and add to outdoor living space
- Elegant master bedroom suite features a five-sided windowed alcove and private deck
- Corner kitchen has a sink-top peninsula
- 4 bedrooms, 2 1/2 baths, 2-car drive under garage
- Basement foundation

## Price Code D

**To order this plan, visit the Menards Building Materials Desk.**

*North Hampton*

## Luxury Home For Narrow Site Has Exciting Interior

2,158 total square feet of living area

### Special features

- Vaulted entry has a coat closet and built-in shelves with plant shelf above
- The two-story living room has tall dramatic windows flanking the fireplace and a full-length second floor balcony
- A laundry and half bath are located near the kitchen which has over 30' of counterspace
- Vaulted master bedroom has window seat entry, two walk-in closets and a luxury bath
- 3 bedrooms, 2 1/2 baths, 2-car garage
- Basement foundation

### Price Code C

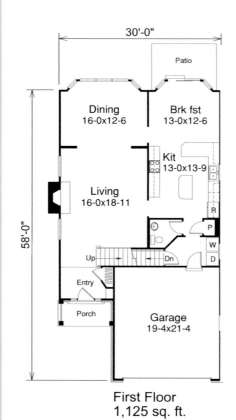

First Floor
1,125 sq. ft.

Second Floor
1,033 sq. ft.

**To order this plan, visit the Menards Building Materials Desk.**

*Kingsmill*

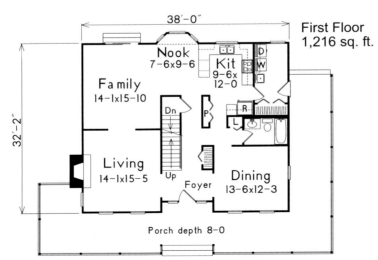

Second Floor
896 sq. ft.

**Br 3**
12-9x12-7

**MBr**
14-1x17-7
vaulted

Dn

skylt

L

open to below

**Br 2**
13-6x11-8
vaulted

38'-0"

First Floor
1,216 sq. ft.

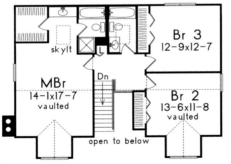

**Nook**
7-6x9-6

**Kit**
9-6x
12-0

D

P O
D
S

W

**Family**
14-1x15-10

Dn

P

R

L

32'-2"

**Living**
14-1x15-5

Up

Foyer

**Dining**
13-6x12-3

Porch depth 8-0

## Attractive Dormers Enhance Facade

2,112 total square feet of living area

### Special features

- Kitchen efficiently connects to the formal dining area
- Nook located between the family room and kitchen creates an ideal breakfast area
- Both baths on the second floor feature skylights
- 3 bedrooms, 3 baths
- Basement foundation, drawings also include crawl space foundation

## Price Code C

**To order this plan, visit the Menards Building Materials Desk.**

*Stonington*

## Stone Decorates Facade

1,838 total square feet of living area

### Special features

- Energy efficient home with 2" x 6" exterior walls
- The angled great room features a corner fireplace, French doors to the rear deck and connects to the dining room for a spacious atmosphere
- The wrap-around kitchen counter offers plenty of workspace and room for casual meals
- Retreat to the master bedroom where a deluxe bath, walk-in closet and deck access will pamper the homeowners
- 3 bedrooms, 2 baths, 2-car garage
- Crawl space foundation, drawings also include basement foundation

### Price Code C

**To order this plan, visit the Menards Building Materials Desk.**

*Mayberry*

## Year-Round Hideaway

416 total square feet of living area

### Special features

- Open floor plan creates a spacious feeling
- Covered porch has rustic appeal
- The kitchen offers plenty of cabinets and workspace
- Large linen closet is centrally located and close to the bath
- 2" x 6" exterior walls available, please order plan #M03-058D-0076
- Sleeping area, 1 bath
- Slab foundation

### Price Code AAA

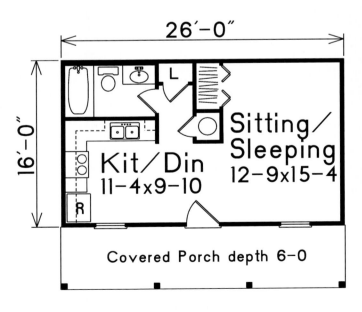

26'-0"

16'-0"

Kit/Din
11-4x9-10

Sitting/
Sleeping
12-9x15-4

L

Covered Porch depth 6-0

*Clarksburg*

## Country Home With Gracious Proportions

2,054 total square feet of living area

### Special features

- A sweeping porch leads to the large foyer with staircase, powder room and handy coat closet
- Spacious living room has a fireplace, triple door to patio and an adjacent computer room
- Kitchen features a snack bar, island counter, pantry and breakfast area with bay window
- Large master bedroom has two spacious closets and accesses a luxury bath with separate toilet and corner tub
- 3 bedrooms, 2 1/2 baths, 2-car detached garage
- Basement foundation

### Price Code C

Second Floor
1,020 sq. ft.

Br 3
12-9x12-8

Dn

MBr
12-6x16-4

Br 2
12-10x13-0

34'-0"

Patio

Brk fst

Living
12-6x20-0

W
D

Dn

Kit
13-0x18-0

30'-0"

Dining
12-8x10-8

Up

Computer
11-0x9-0

Porch depth 6-4

First Floor
1,034 sq. ft.

**To order this plan, visit the Menards Building Materials Desk.**

*Waterbury*

## Special Planning In This Compact Home

977 total square feet of living area

### Special features

■ Comfortable living room features a vaulted ceiling, fireplace, plant shelf and coat closet
■ Both bedrooms are located on the second floor and share a bath with double-bowl vanity and linen closet
■ Sliding glass doors in the dining room provide access to the deck
■ 2 bedrooms, 1 1/2 baths, 1-car garage
■ Basement foundation

### Price Code A

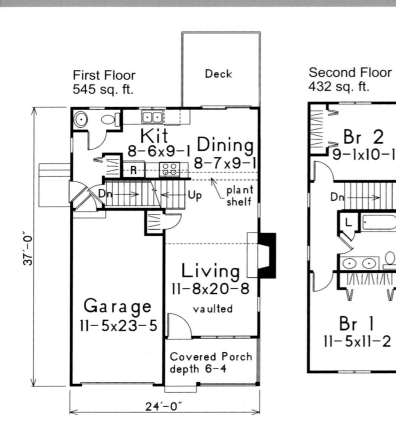

First Floor
545 sq. ft.

Deck

Kit
8-6x9-1

Dining
8-7x9-1

R

Dn

Up

plant shelf

Living
11-8x20-8
vaulted

Garage
11-5x23-5

Covered Porch
depth 6-4

37'-0"

24'-0"

Second Floor
432 sq. ft.

Br 2
9-1x10-1

Dn

L

Br 1
11-5x11-2

Garden furniture can be found in a variety of materials. Consider the pros and cons of each before selecting. Wicker has a traditional look and moderate cost but needs protection from weather. Metal is highly durable, usually needs cushions and can be cold to the touch. Resin is an inexpensive and light material and is easily cleaned with soap and water. Weather-resistant hardwood can be left natural for low maintenance and is durable but costly. Regular hardwood or treated softwood is inexpensive but will need regular painting or staining.

*Lakepoint*

## Dramatic Look For Quiet Hideaway

1,750 total square feet of living area

### Special features

- The family room is brightened by floor-to-ceiling windows and sliding doors providing access to a large deck
- Second floor sitting area is perfect for a game room or entertaining
- Kitchen includes eat-in dining area plus outdoor dining patio as a bonus
- Plenty of closet and storage space throughout
- 3 bedrooms, 2 baths
- Basement foundation, drawings also include crawl space and slab foundations

### Price Code B

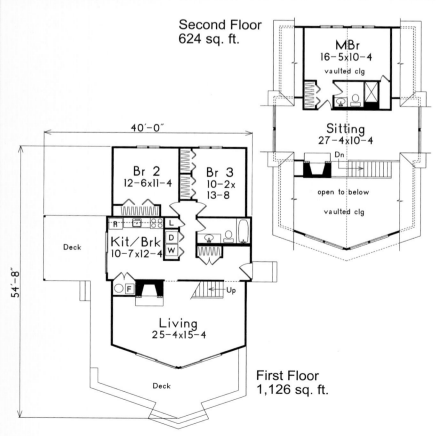

Second Floor
624 sq. ft.

MBr
16-5x10-4
vaulted clg

Sitting
27-4x10-4

Dn

open to below

vaulted clg

40'-0"

Br 2
12-6x11-4

Br 3
10-2x
13-8

Deck

Kit/Brk
10-7x12-4

54'-8"

Up

Living
25-4x15-4

Deck

First Floor
1,126 sq. ft.

124

**To order this plan, visit the Menards Building Materials Desk.**

*Vandora*

**Second Floor**
**1,240 sq. ft.**

Br 1
11-10x10-7

Kit/Brk
14-10x10-10

R

P

Dn

Sitting
15-0x16-1

L

Br 2
11-9x10-8

Sloped Ceiling

34'-0"

**First Floor**

W. Furn.

Utility

Garage
23-2x27-0
9' Ceiling

D

W

S

Up

32'-0"

9'x8' Door        9'x8' Door

6'x4' Porch

## 2-Car Garage Apartment

1,240 total square feet of living area

### Special features

- Kitchen/breakfast area combine for added spaciousness
- Sloped ceiling adds appeal in the sitting area
- The utilities are located on the lower level
- 2 bedrooms, 1 bath, 2-car garage
- Basement foundation

### Price Code AAA

**To order this plan, visit the Menards Building Materials Desk.**

**MENARDS**®

*Littleton*

## Three-Way Design

588 total square feet of living area

### Special features

- May be built as a duplex, 4-car garage or apartment garage/vacation cabin as shown
- Very livable plan in a small footprint
- Living room features a functional entry, bayed dining area, corner fireplace and opens to kitchen with breakfast bar
- 1 bedroom, 1 bath, 2-car side entry garage
- Slab foundation
- 1,176 square feet of living area when built as a duplex

### Price Code AAA

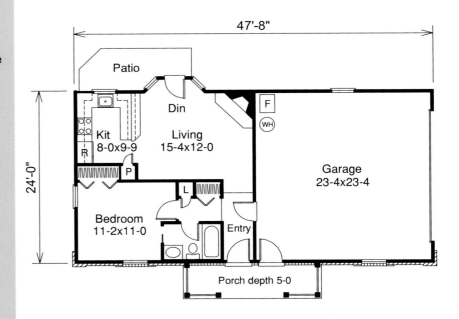

47'-8"

24'-0"

Patio

Din

Kit
8-0x9-9

Living
15-4x12-0

F

WH

R

P

Garage
23-4x23-4

L

Bedroom
11-2x11-0

Entry

Porch depth 5-0

**To order this plan, visit the Menards Building Materials Desk.**

*Livingston*

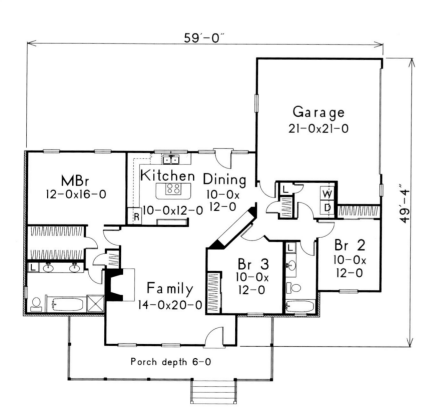

## Covered Porch Is Focal Point Of Entry

1,595 total square feet of living area

### Special features

- Dining room has a convenient built-in desk and provides access to the outdoors
- L-shaped kitchen features an island cooktop
- Family room has a high ceiling and fireplace
- Private master bedroom includes a large walk-in closet and bath with separate tub and shower units
- 3 bedrooms, 2 baths, 2-car side entry garage
- Slab foundation, drawings also include crawl space foundation

**Price Code B**

*Waterview*

## Superb Vacation Style

1,278 total square feet of living area

### Special features

- Energy efficient home with 2" x 6" exterior walls
- Enter this home to find a two-story great room topped with skylights that offer a dramatic first impression
- The screened porch extends dining opportunites and provides a lovely space to enjoy the outdoors year round
- The second floor master bedroom includes a private deck for the ultimate in relaxation
- 2 bedrooms, 1 1/2 baths
- Basement foundation

### Price Code A

Second Floor
518 sq. ft.

First Floor
760 sq. ft.

**To order this plan, visit the Menards Building Materials® Desk.**

# Plan #M03-008D-0094

*Edgewater*

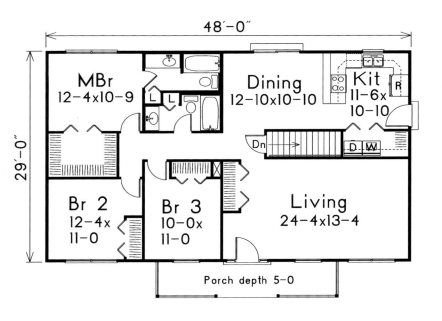

## Efficient Ranch With Country Charm

1,364 total square feet of living area

### Special features

- Master bedroom features a spacious walk-in closet and private bath
- Living room is highlighted with several windows
- Kitchen with snack bar is adjacent to the dining area
- Plenty of storage space throughout
- 3 bedrooms, 2 baths, optional 2-car garage
- Basement foundation, drawings also include crawl space foundation

**Price Code A**

**To order this plan, visit the Menards Building Materials Desk.**

## Rosehill

# A Cottage With Class

576 total square feet of living area

### Special features

- Perfect country retreat features vaulted living room and entry with skylights and a plant shelf above
- A double-door entry leads to the vaulted bedroom with bath access
- Kitchen offers generous storage and pass-through breakfast bar
- 1 bedroom, 1 bath
- Crawl space foundation

### Price Code AAA

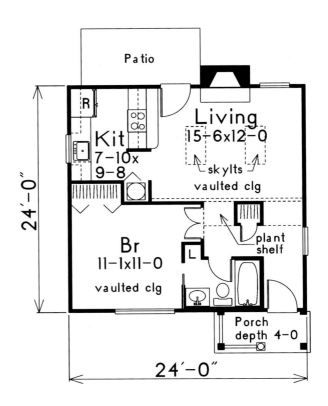

**To order this plan, visit the Menards Building Materials Desk.**

*Addison*

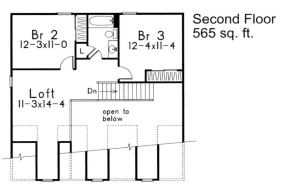

Second Floor
565 sq. ft.

Br 2
12-3x11-0

Br 3
12-4x11-4

L

Loft
11-3x14-4

Dn

open to
below

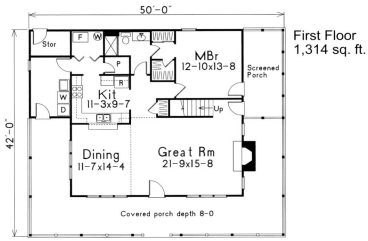

50'-0"

42'-0"

Stor

F   W

MBr
12-10x13-8

Screened
Porch

P

R

Kit
11-3x9-7

W

D

Up

Dining
11-7x14-4

Great Rm
21-9x15-8

Covered porch depth 8-0

First Floor
1,314 sq. ft.

# Charming Wrap-Around Porch

1,879 total square feet of living area

## Special features

- Open floor plan on both floors makes home appear larger
- Loft area overlooks great room or can become an optional fourth bedroom
- Large storage in rear of home has access from exterior
- 3 bedrooms, 2 baths
- Crawl space foundation

## Price Code C

**To order this plan, visit the Menards Building Materials Desk.**

*Leawood*

## Ornate Corner Porch Catches The Eye

1,550 total square feet of living area

### Special features

- Impressive front entrance with a wrap-around covered porch and raised foyer
- Corner fireplace provides a focal point in the vaulted great room
- Loft is easily converted to a third bedroom or activity center
- Large kitchen/family room includes greenhouse windows and access to the deck and utility area
- The secondary bedroom has a large dormer and window seat
- 2 bedrooms, 2 1/2 baths, 2-car garage
- Basement foundation

### Price Code B

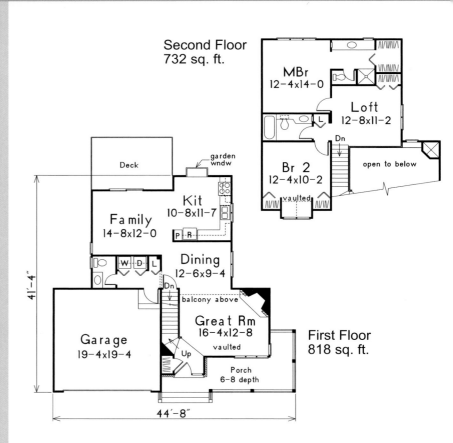

Second Floor
732 sq. ft.

MBr
12-4x14-0

Loft
12-8x11-2

Br 2
12-4x10-2

open to below

vaulted

Deck

garden wndw

Kit
10-8x11-7

Family
14-8x12-0

Dining
12-6x9-4

balcony above

Great Rm
16-4x12-8
vaulted

Garage
19-4x19-4

Up

Porch
6-8 depth

First Floor
818 sq. ft.

41'-4"

44'-8"

**To order this plan, visit the Menards Building Materials Desk.**

*Lakeland*

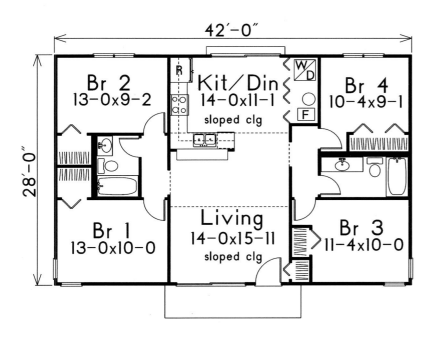

## Clerestory Windows Enhance Home's Facade

1,176 total square feet of living area

### Special features

- Efficient kitchen offers plenty of storage, a dining area and a stylish eating bar
- A gathering space is created by the large central living room
- Closet and storage space throughout helps keep sporting equipment organized and easily accessible
- Each end of the home is comprised of two bedrooms and a full bath
- 4 bedrooms, 2 baths
- Crawl space foundation, drawings also include slab foundation

### Price Code AA

*Southwood*

## Recessed Stone Entry Provides A Unique Accent

717 total square feet of living area

### Special features

- Incline ladder leads up to cozy loft area
- Living room features plenty of windows and a vaulted ceiling
- U-shaped kitchen includes a small bay window at the sink
- 1 bedroom, 1 bath
- Slab foundation

### Price Code AAA

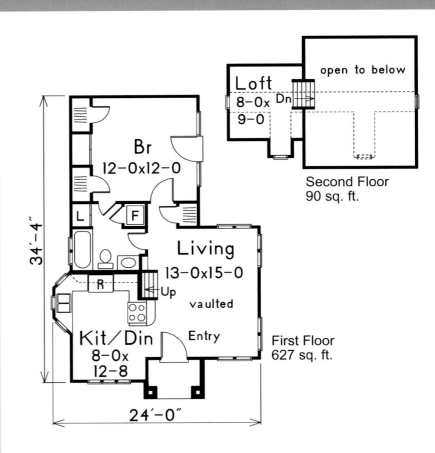

Loft
8-0x
9-0

open to below

Dn

Second Floor
90 sq. ft.

Br
12-0x12-0

L    F

Living
13-0x15-0

Up

vaulted

R

Kit/Din
8-0x
12-8

Entry

First Floor
627 sq. ft.

34'-4"

24'-0"

**To order this plan, visit the Menards Building Materials Desk.**

*Tahoe*

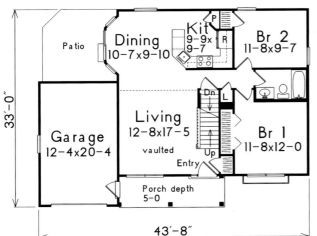

Second Floor
446 sq. ft.

Br 4
11-0x13-0

Br 3
14-0x9-7

Dn
L

open to
below

Storage Area
14-0x12-0

First Floor
884 sq. ft.

Patio

Dining
10-7x9-10

Kit
9-9x
9-7

P
R

Br 2
11-8x9-7

Dn
L

33'-0"

Garage
12-4x20-4

Living
12-8x17-5
vaulted

Up

Br 1
11-8x12-0

Entry

Porch depth
5-0

43'-8"

## Openness Reflects Relaxed Lifestyle

1,330 total square feet of living area

### Special features

- Vaulted living room is open to the bayed dining room and kitchen creating an ideal space for entertaining
- Two bedrooms, a bath and linen closet complete the first floor and are easily accessible
- The second floor offers two bedrooms with walk-in closets, a very large storage room and an opening with louvered doors which overlooks the living room
- 4 bedrooms, 2 baths, 1-car garage
- Basement foundation

### Price Code A

Maintaining a central air conditioner is easy if you follow the steps below. First, keep the condensing unit clear for airflow. Hose out leaves and keep shrubs pruned back. Second, during humid weather, check the condesate drain to be sure that it is carrying off excess moisture. Last, a clogged filter can shut down a unit. Change filters several times per season; never run a system without a filter.

## *Montview*

## Stylish A-Frame Home

1,117 total square feet of living area

### Special features

- Energy efficient home with 2" x 6" exterior walls
- A wide deck opens to the combined living room and kitchen/breakfast area that span two-stories high
- Windows flood this vacation home with an abundance of light, keeping the area bright and cheerful
- The second floor loft offers a spacious area perfect for a play room or home theater
- 2 bedrooms, 1 bath
- Basement foundation

### Price Code AA

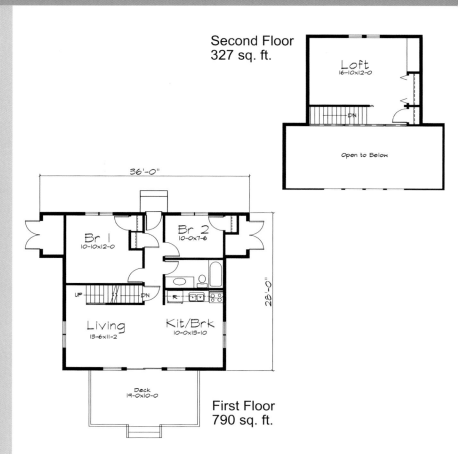

Second Floor
327 sq. ft.

Loft
16-10x12-0

Open to Below

36'-0"

Br 1
10-10x12-0

Br 2
10-0x7-6

28'-0"

UP    DN

Living
13-6x11-2

Kit/Brk
10-0x13-10

Deck
19-0x10-0

First Floor
790 sq. ft.

**To order this plan, visit the Menards Building Materials Desk.**

*Fairfax*

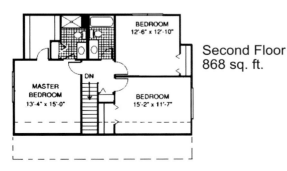

Second Floor
868 sq. ft.

BEDROOM
12'-6" x 12'-10"

MASTER
BEDROOM
13'-4" x 15'-0"

DN

BEDROOM
15'-2" x 11'-7"

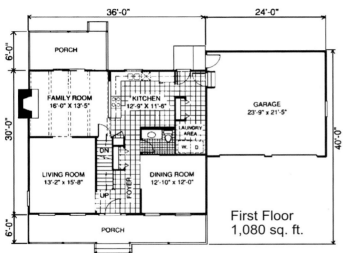

36'-0"    24'-0"

6'-0"

PORCH

30'-0"

FAMILY ROOM
16'-0" X 13'-5"

KITCHEN
12'-9" X 11'-6"

GARAGE
23'-9" x 21'-5"

40'-0"

LAUNDRY
AREA

W  D

DN

LIVING ROOM
13'-2" x 15'-8"

DINING ROOM
12'-10" x 12'-0"

UP

FOYER

6'-0"

PORCH

First Floor
1,080 sq. ft.

## Inviting Home With Country Flavor

1,948 total square feet of living area

### Special features

- Large elongated porch for moonlit evenings
- Stylish family room features a beamed ceiling
- Skillfully designed kitchen is convenient to an oversized laundry area
- Second floor bedrooms are all generously sized
- 3 bedrooms, 2 1/2 baths, 2-car garage
- Basement foundation, drawings also include crawl space foundation

## Price Code C

**To order this plan, visit the Menards Building Materials Desk.**

## Winterknoll

## Open Floor Plan

1,217 total square feet of living area

### Special features

- Everyone will be amazed as they enter this home to view a wide open living area comprised of the family room and breakfast/kitchen, all topped with a vaulted ceiling
- The master bedroom is fit for relaxing with a private bath and walk-in closet
- The garage enters the home through the extra-large laundry room with enough space for storage
- 2 bedrooms, 2 baths, 2-car garage
- Basement foundation

### Price Code D

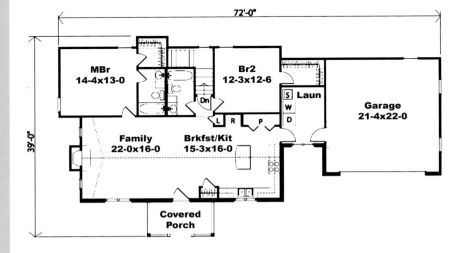

To order this plan, visit the Menards Building Materials Desk.

*Lakeview*

## Summer Home Or Year-Round

1,403 total square feet of living area

### Special features

- Impressive living areas for a modest-sized home
- Special master/hall bath has linen storage, step-up tub and lots of window light
- Spacious closets everywhere you look
- 3 bedrooms, 2 baths, 2-car drive under garage
- Basement foundation

### Price Code A

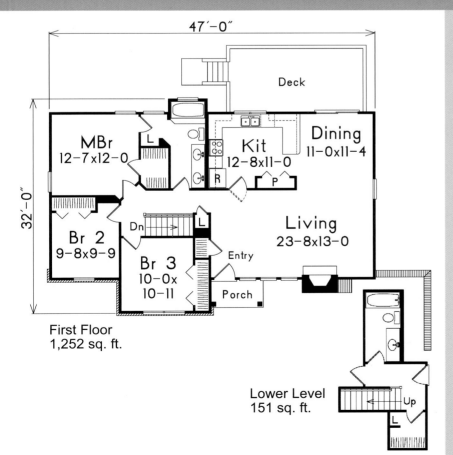

First Floor
1,252 sq. ft.

Lower Level
151 sq. ft.

*Timberbrooke*

## Charming Exterior And Cozy Interior

1,127 total square feet of living area

### Special features

- Plant shelf joins kitchen and dining room
- Vaulted master bedroom has double walk-in closets, deck access and a private bath
- Great room features a vaulted ceiling, fireplace and sliding doors to the covered deck
- Ideal home for a narrow lot
- 2 bedrooms, 2 baths, 2-car garage
- Basement foundation

### Price Code AA

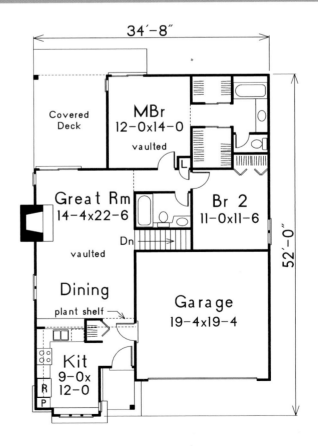

34'-8"

52'-0"

Covered Deck

MBr
12-0x14-0
vaulted

Great Rm
14-4x22-6

Br 2
11-0x11-6

Dn

vaulted

Dining

plant shelf

Garage
19-4x19-4

Kit
9-0x
12-0

R
P

**To order this plan, visit the Menards Building Materials® Desk.**

# Plan #M03-008D-0143

*Kingsport*

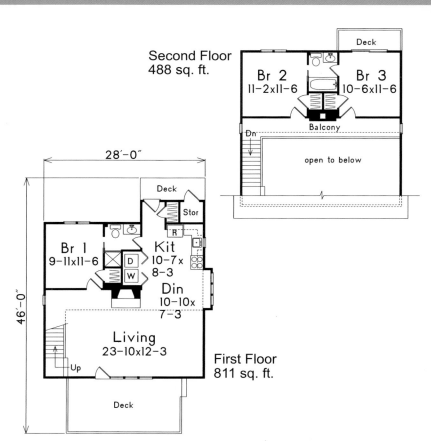

Second Floor
488 sq. ft.

Deck

Br 2
11-2x11-6

Br 3
10-6x11-6

Dn

Balcony

open to below

28'-0"

Deck

Stor

R

Br 1
9-11x11-6

Kit
10-7x
8-3

D
W

Din
10-10x
7-3

46'-0"

Living
23-10x12-3

Up

First Floor
811 sq. ft.

Deck

## Breathtaking Balcony Overlook

1,299 total square feet of living area

### Special features

- Convenient storage for skis, etc. is located outside the front entrance
- The kitchen and dining room receive light from the box-bay window
- Large vaulted living room features a cozy fireplace and overlook from the second floor balcony
- Two second floor bedrooms share a Jack and Jill bath
- Second floor balcony extends over the entire length of the living room below
- 3 bedrooms, 2 baths
- Crawl space foundation, drawings also include slab foundation

### Price Code A

**To order this plan, visit the Menards Building Materials Desk.**

141

## Chesapeake

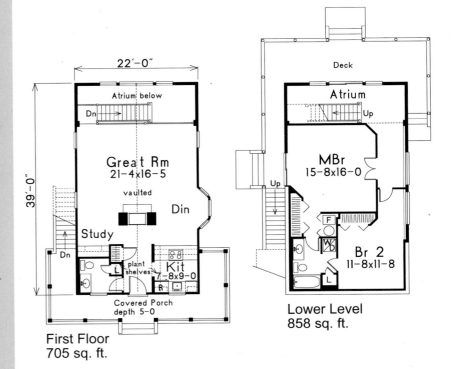

Rear View

# Irresistible Paradise Retreat

1,563 total square feet of living area

### Special features

- Enjoyable wrap-around porch and lower sundeck
- Vaulted entry is adorned with a palladian window, plant shelves, stone floor and fireplace
- Huge vaulted great room has a magnificent view through a two-story atrium window wall
- 2 bedrooms, 1 1/2 baths
- Walk-out basement foundation

### Price Code B

First Floor
705 sq. ft.

Lower Level
858 sq. ft.

**To order this plan, visit the Menards Building Materials Desk.**

*Sutton*

## Vaulted Ceiling Adds Spaciousness

990 total square feet of living area

### Special features

- Energy efficient home with 2" x 6" exterior walls
- Wrap-around porch creates a relaxing retreat
- Combined family and dining rooms boast a vaulted ceiling
- Space for an efficiency washer and dryer unit offers convenience
- 2 bedrooms, 1 bath
- Crawl space foundation

### Price Code AA

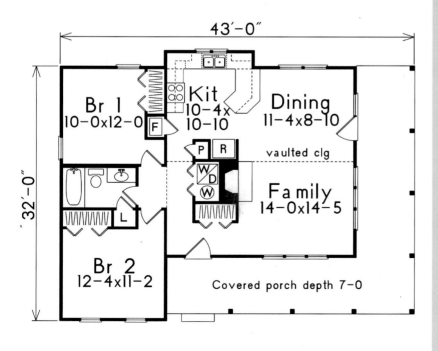

43'-0"

32'-0"

Br 1
10-0x12-0

Kit
10-4x
10-10

Dining
11-4x8-10

vaulted clg

Family
14-0x14-5

Br 2
12-4x11-2

Covered porch depth 7-0

*Thornwood*

## Front Porch Adds Style To This Ranch

1,496 total square feet of living area

### Special features

- Master bedroom features a tray ceiling, walk-in closet and spacious bath
- Vaulted ceiling and fireplace grace the family room
- Dining room is adjacent to the kitchen and features access to the rear porch
- Convenient access to the utility room from the kitchen
- 3 bedrooms, 2 baths, 2-car drive under garage
- Basement foundation

### Price Code A

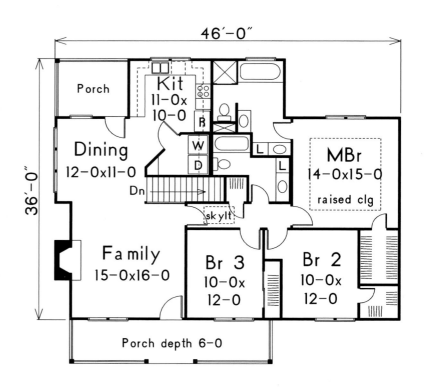

**To order this plan, visit the Menards Building Materials Desk.**

*Rosevale*

## Economize Without Sacrifice

960 total square feet of living area

### Special features

- Attractive appearance adds to any neighborhood
- A nice-sized living room leads to an informal family area with eat-in L-shaped kitchen, access to rear yard and basement space
- Three bedrooms with lots of closet space and a convenient hall bath complete the home
- 3 bedrooms, 1 bath
- Basement foundation, drawings also include crawl space and slab foundations

### Price Code AA

**FLOOR PLAN**

40'-0"

24'-0"

BEDROOM 11'-4" x 11'

BATH

FAMILY - KITCHEN 18'-6" x 11'

dn.

L. C.

C.

BED ROOM 11'-2" x 9'-4"

C

C

BED ROOM 9'-4" x 8'-4"

LIVING ROOM 15'-2" x 11'-8"

**To order this plan, visit the Menards Building Materials Desk.**

145

*Shasta*

## Sensational Cottage Retreat

647 total square feet of living area

### Special features

- Large vaulted room for living/sleeping has plant shelves on each end, stone fireplace and wide glass doors for views
- Roomy kitchen is vaulted and has a bayed dining area and fireplace
- Step down into a sunken and vaulted bath featuring a 6'-0" whirlpool tub-in-a-bay with shelves at each end for storage
- A large palladian window adorns each end of the cottage giving a cheery atmosphere throughout
- 1 living/sleeping room, 1 bath
- Crawl space foundation

### Price Code AAA

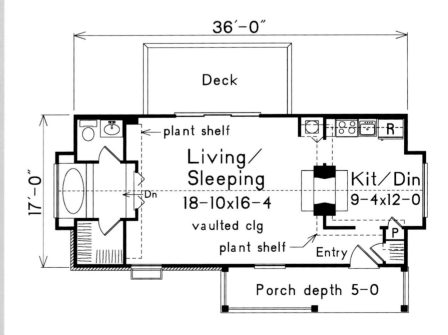

**To order this plan, visit the Menards Building Materials Desk.**

*Maxwell*

## Cheerful Cottage

665 total square feet of living area

### Special features

- Spacious breakfast/sitting area flows into kitchen area
- A stacked washer and dryer adds convenience to this cottage home
- A coat closet at the entry and a pantry in the kitchen provide essential storage space
- 1 bedroom, 1 bath, 1-car garage
- Slab foundation

### Price Code AAA

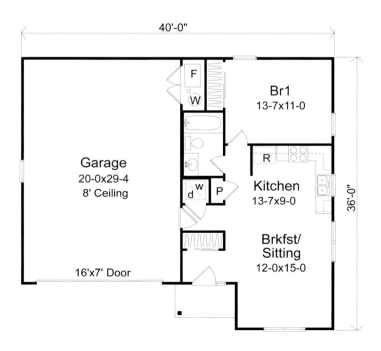

40'-0"

Garage
20-0x29-4
8' Ceiling

16'x7' Door

F

W

Br1
13-7x11-0

R

d w P

Kitchen
13-7x9-0

Brkfst/
Sitting
12-0x15-0

36'-0"

*Foxbriar*

## Compact, Convenient And Charming

1,266 total square feet of living area

### Special features

- Energy efficient home with 2" x 6" exterior walls
- Narrow frontage is perfect for small lots
- Prominent central hall provides a convenient connection for all main rooms
- Design incorporates full-size master bedroom complete with dressing room, bath and walk-in closet
- Angled kitchen includes handy laundry facilities and is adjacent to an oversized storage area
- 3 bedrooms, 2 baths, 2-car rear entry garage
- Crawl space foundation, drawings also include slab foundation

**Price Code A**

Garage
21-4x21-2

Stor
9-8x6-6

Br 2
10-4x11-4

Br 3
10-4x11-4

Dining
9-6x
11-6

Kit
8-2x
15-0

Living
17-4x17-6

MBr
10-6x14-10

Entry

64'-0"

Porch depth 6-0

40'-0"

**To order this plan, visit the Menards Building Materials Desk.**

*Juneau*

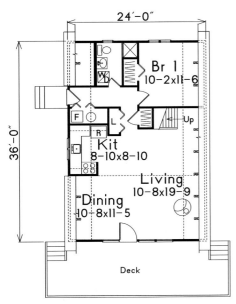

24'-0"

36'-0"

Br 1
10-2x11-6

Kit
8-10x8-10

F

L

R

Up

Living
10-8x19-9

Dining
10-8x11-5

Deck

**First Floor**
864 sq. ft.

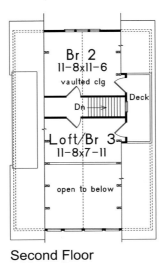

Br 2
11-8x11-6
vaulted clg

Dn

Deck

Loft/Br 3
11-8x7-11

open to below

**Second Floor**
360 sq. ft.

## Fantastic
## A-Frame Get-Away

1,224 total square feet of living area

### Special features

- Get away to this cozy A-frame featuring three bedrooms
- Living and dining rooms with free-standing fireplace walk out onto a large deck
- U-shaped kitchen has a unique built-in table at the end of the counter for intimate gatherings
- Both second floor bedrooms enjoy their own private balcony
- 3 bedrooms, 1 bath
- Crawl space foundation

## Price Code A

*Bridgefield*

## Apartment Garage With Atrium

902 total square feet of living area

### Special features

- Vaulted entry with laundry room leads to a spacious second floor apartment
- The large living room features an entry coat closet, L-shaped kitchen with pantry and dining area/balcony overlooking atrium window wall
- Roomy bedroom with walk-in closet is convenient to hall bath
- 1 bedroom, 1 bath, 2-car side entry garage
- Slab foundation

### Price Code AA

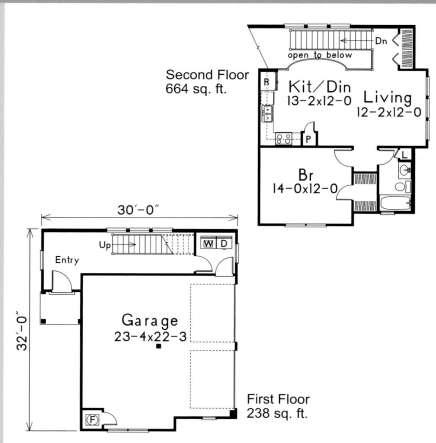

Second Floor
664 sq. ft.

Kit/Din
13-2x12-0

Living
12-2x12-0

Br
14-0x12-0

30'-0"

32'-0"

Up

Entry

W D

Garage
23-4x22-3

First Floor
238 sq. ft.

**To order this plan, visit the Menards Building Materials Desk.**

*Arrowhead*

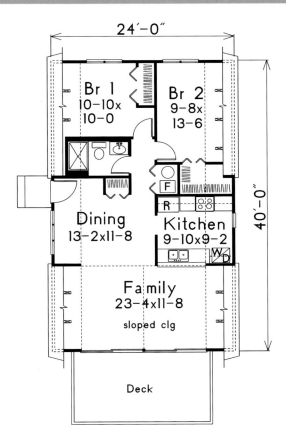

## Vacation Paradise

960 total square feet of living area

### Special features

- Interesting roof and wood beams overhang a generous-sized deck
- Family room is vaulted and opens to the dining area and kitchen
- Pullman-style kitchen has been skillfully designed
- Two bedrooms and hall bath are located at the rear of home
- 2 bedrooms, 1 bath
- Crawl space foundation

### Price Code AA

*Pinetrail*

## Delightful Vacation Retreat

751 total square feet of living area

### Special features

- The covered porch expands the entire width of this charming cottage
- The kitchen/dining area and sitting nook combine for increased spaciousness
- Two bedrooms share a roomy bath
- 2" x 6" exterior walls available, please order plan #M03-058D-0131
- 2 bedrooms, 1 bath
- Crawl space foundation

### Price Code AAA

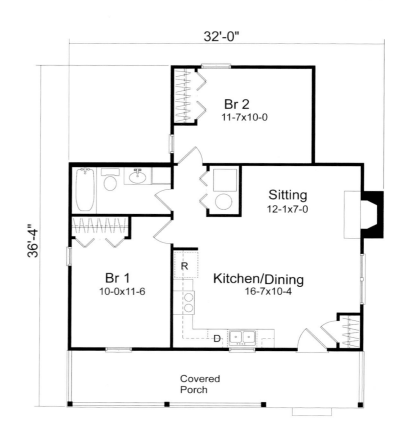

Br 2
11-7x10-0

Sitting
12-1x7-0

Br 1
10-0x11-6

Kitchen/Dining
16-7x10-4

Covered Porch

32'-0"

36'-4"

**To order this plan, visit the Menards Building Materials Desk.**

*Mapleville*

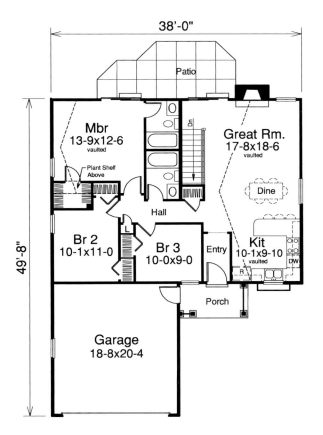

38'-0"

Patio

Mbr
13-9x12-6
vaulted

Plant Shelf
Above

Great Rm.
17-8x18-6
vaulted

Dn

Dine

Hall

Br 2
10-1x11-0

L

Br 3
10-0x9-0

Entry

Kit
10-1x9-10
vaulted

DW

R

49'-8"

Porch

Garage
18-8x20-4

## The Ideal Affordable Home

1,102 total square feet of living area

### Special features

- Attractive exterior features a cozy porch, palladian windows and a decorative planter box
- The vaulted great room has a fireplace, view to rear patio and dining area with feature window
- Open to the great room is a U-shaped kitchen which includes all the necessities and a breakfast bar
- The master bedroom offers a vaulted ceiling, private bath, walk-in closet and sliding doors to the rear patio
- 3 bedrooms, 2 baths, 2-car garage
- Basement foundation, drawings also include slab and crawl space foundations

**Price Code AA**

**To order this plan, visit the Menards Building Materials Desk.**

*Hillsdale*

## Country Retreat For Quiet Times

**1,211 total square feet of living area**

### Special features

- Extraordinary views are enjoyed in the vaulted family room through sliding doors
- Functional kitchen features snack bar and laundry closet
- Bedroom and bunk room complete first floor while a large bedroom with two storage areas and balcony complete the second floor
- Additional plan for second floor creates 223 square feet of additional bedroom space
- 2 bedrooms, 1 bath
- Crawl space foundation, drawings also include basement foundation

### Price Code A

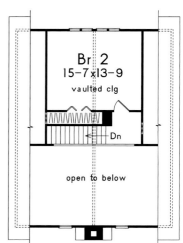

Second Floor
327 sq. ft.

Br 2
15-7 x 13-9
vaulted clg

Dn

open to below

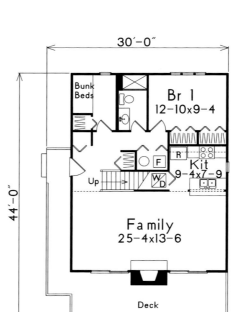

30'-0"

Bunk Beds

Br 1
12-10x9-4

Kit
9-4x7-9

R

F

W D

Up

Family
25-4x13-6

44'-0"

Deck

First Floor
884 sq. ft.

**To order this plan, visit the Menards Building Materials Desk.**

*Siminridge*

## Compact Home For Sloping Lot

1,332 total square feet of living area

### Special features

- Home offers both basement and first floor entry locations
- A dramatic living room features a vaulted ceiling, fireplace, exterior balcony and dining area
- An L-shaped kitchen offers spacious cabinetry, breakfast area with bay window and access to the rear patio
- 3 bedrooms, 2 baths, 4-car tandem garage
- Walk-out basement foundation

### Price Code A

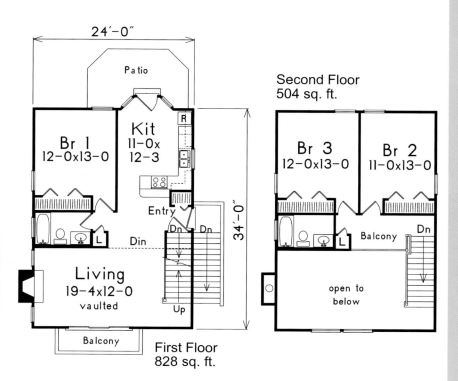

24'-0"

Patio

Br 1
12-0x13-0

Kit
11-0x
12-3

Entry

Din

Living
19-4x12-0
vaulted

Balcony

Dn Dn

Up

34'-0"

**First Floor**
828 sq. ft.

**Second Floor**
504 sq. ft.

Br 3
12-0x13-0

Br 2
11-0x13-0

Balcony

Dn

open to below

Sycamore Hill

## Ideal Home Or Retirement Retreat

1,013 total square feet of living area

### Special features

- Energy efficient home with 2" x 6" exterior walls
- Vaulted ceilings in both the family room and kitchen with dining area just beyond the breakfast bar
- Plant shelf above kitchen is a special feature
- Oversized utility room has space for a full-size washer and dryer
- Hall bath is centrally located with easy access from both bedrooms
- 2 bedrooms, 1 bath
- Slab foundation

**Price Code AA**

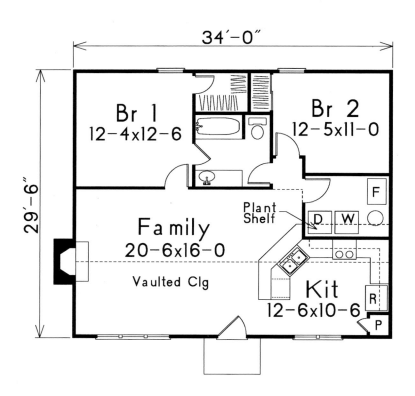

**To order this plan, visit the Menards Building Materials Desk.**

**MENARDS**®

*Oaktrail*

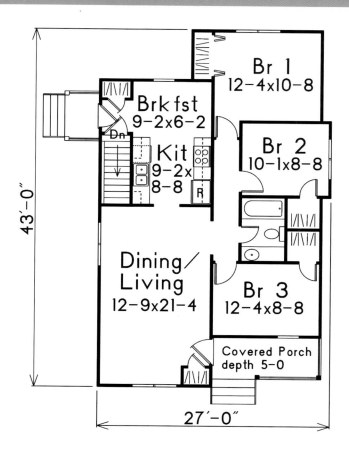

## Compact Home Maximizes Space

987 total square feet of living area

### Special features

- Galley kitchen opens into the cozy breakfast room
- Convenient coat closets are located by both entrances
- Dining/living room offers an expansive open area
- Breakfast room has access to the outdoors
- Front porch is great for enjoying outdoor living
- 3 bedrooms, 1 bath
- Basement foundation

### Price Code AA

**To order this plan, visit the Menards Building Materials Desk.**

*Brookview*

## Country Appeal For A Small Lot

1,299 total square feet of living area

### Special features

- Large porch for enjoying relaxing evenings
- First floor master bedroom has a bay window, walk-in closet and roomy bath
- Two generous bedrooms with lots of closet space, a hall bath, linen closet and balcony overlook comprise the second floor
- 3 bedrooms, 2 1/2 baths
- Basement foundation

### Price Code A

24'-0"

Patio

P

R

Kit
12-0x14-10

MBr
13-0x13-6

40'-0"

Dn

Living Rm
12-1x18-3

Up

L

L

Porch depth 6-0

First Floor
834 sq. ft.

Second Floor
465 sq. ft.

Br 2
12-0x12-6

Br 3
11-0x12-6

open to below

Dn

L

**To order this plan, visit the Menards Building Materials Desk.**

*Woodside*

## Mountain Retreat

1,209 total square feet of living area

### Special features

- Bracketed shed roof and ski storage add charm to this vacation home
- Living and dining rooms enjoy a sloped ceiling, second floor balcony overlook and view to a large deck
- Kitchen features a snack bar and access to the second floor via a circular staircase
- Second floor includes two bedrooms with sizable closets, center hall bath and balcony overlooking rooms below
- 3 bedrooms, 2 baths
- Crawl space foundation

### Price Code A

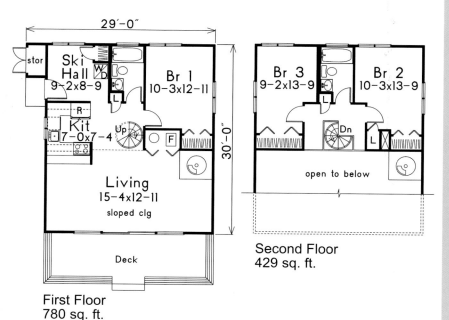

First Floor
780 sq. ft.

Second Floor
429 sq. ft.

*Hillsborough*

## Affordable Four Bedroom Ranch

1,203 total square feet of living area

### Special features

- Large porch for quiet evening relaxation
- The living room features a vaulted ceiling, fireplace and dining area with patio views
- The kitchen includes an abundance of cabinet storage, a large walk-in pantry and door to the rear yard
- The master bedroom has a vaulted ceiling, private bath with built-in linen storage and a walk-in closet
- 4 bedrooms, 2 1/2 baths, 2-car garage
- Basement foundation, drawings also include slab and crawl space foundations

### Price Code A

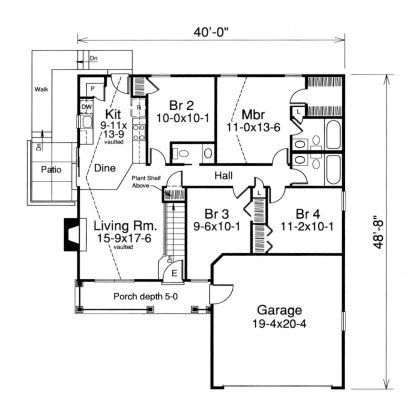

**To order this plan, visit the Menards Building Materials Desk.**

# Plan #M03-058D-0144

**MENARDS**®

*Cranford*

30'-0"

28'-0"

Kitchen
8-4x7

Dining
13x10-4

MBr.
12x10-9

Great Room
13x11

**Second Floor**
701 sq. ft.

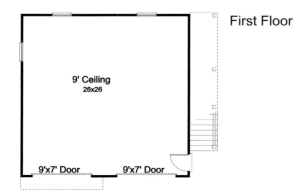

9' Ceiling
26x26

9'x7' Door    9'x7' Door

**First Floor**

## 2-Car Garage Apartment

701 total square feet of living area

### Special features

- Covered stairs lead into the living area
- The open floor plan adds spaciousness
- The utility room has space for a washer and dryer and storage
- 1 bedroom, 1 bath, 2-car garage
- Basement foundation

### Price Code AAA

**To order this plan, visit the Menards Building Materials Desk.**

161

*Westover*

## Compact Home, Perfect Fit For Narrow Lot

1,085 total square feet of living area

### Special features

- Rear porch provides handy access through the kitchen
- Convenient hall linen closet is located on the second floor
- Breakfast bar in the kitchen offers additional counterspace
- Living and dining rooms combine for open living
- 3 bedrooms, 2 baths
- Basement foundation

### Price Code AA

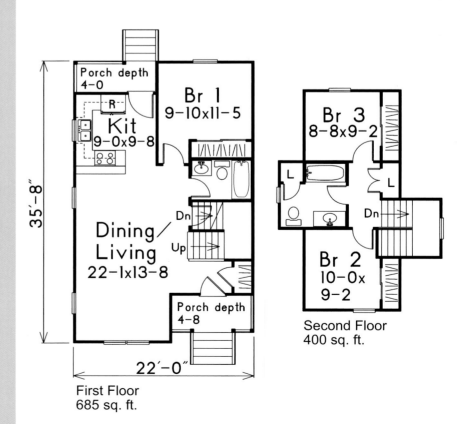

Second Floor
400 sq. ft.

First Floor
685 sq. ft.

162

**To order this plan, visit the Menards Building Materials Desk.**

*Ashridge*

## Atrium Living For Views On A Narrow Lot

1,231 total square feet of living area

### Special features

- Dutch gables and stone accents provide an enchanting appearance
- The spacious living room offers a masonry fireplace, atrium with window wall and is open to a dining area with bay window
- Kitchen has a breakfast counter, lots of cabinet space and glass sliding doors to a balcony
- 380 square feet of optional living area on the lower level
- 2 bedrooms, 2 baths, 1-car drive under rear entry garage
- Walk-out basement foundation

**Price Code A**

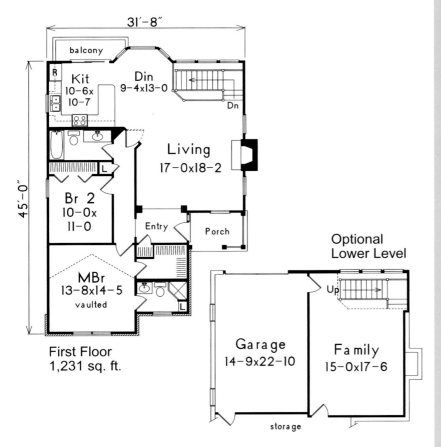

First Floor
1,231 sq. ft.

Optional Lower Level

*Lakeshire*

## Charming Home With Great Privacy

2,445 total square feet of living area

### Special features

- Sunken living room has a corner fireplace, vaulted ceiling and is adjacent to the dining room for entertaining large groups
- Large vaulted open foyer with triple skylights provides an especially bright entry
- Loft area overlooks foyer and features a decorative display area
- Bedrooms are located on the second floor for privacy and convenience, with a vaulted ceiling in the master bedroom
- 4 bedrooms, 2 1/2 baths, 3-car garage
- Basement foundation

### Price Code E

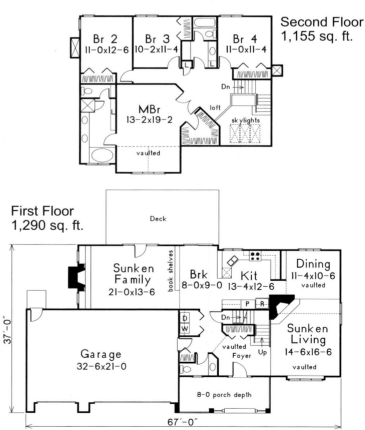

Second Floor 1,155 sq. ft.

Br 2 11-0x12-6
Br 3 10-2x11-4
Br 4 11-0x11-4
MBr 13-2x19-2
loft
Dn
skylights
vaulted

First Floor 1,290 sq. ft.

Deck
Sunken Family 21-0x13-6
book shelves
Brk 8-0x9-0
Kit 13-4x12-6
Dining 11-4x10-6 vaulted
Garage 32-6x21-0
Dn
vaulted Foyer
Up
Sunken Living 14-6x16-6 vaulted
8-0 porch depth
37'-0"
67'-0"

**To order this plan, visit the Menards Building Materials Desk.**

*Grantview*

## Unique A-Frame Detailing Has Appeal

1,272 total square feet of living area

### Special features

- Stone fireplace accents living room
- Spacious kitchen includes snack bar overlooking the living room
- First floor bedroom is roomy and secluded
- Plenty of closetspace for second floor bedrooms plus a generous balcony which wraps around the second floor
- 3 bedrooms, 1 1/2 baths
- Crawl space foundation

### Price Code A

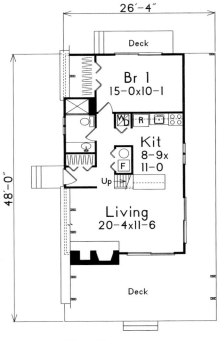

26'-4"

Deck

Br 1
15-0x10-1

Kit
8-9x
11-0

Living
20-4x11-6

48'-0"

Deck

First Floor
792 sq. ft.

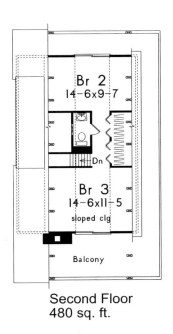

Br 2
14-6x9-7

Dn

Br 3
14-6x11-5
sloped clg

Balcony

Second Floor
480 sq. ft.

*Cortez*

# Exciting, Combined Living Spaces

1,559 total square feet of living area

## Special features

- Energy efficient home with 2" x 6" exterior walls
- This stylish earth berm design features stunning planter boxes surrounding the home
- Enjoy the spacious atmosphere created with the combined kitchen, living and dining rooms
- Retreat to the master bedroom to find a dressing area with two closets and a private bath with double-bowl vanity
- 3 bedrooms, 2 baths
- Slab foundation

## Price Code B

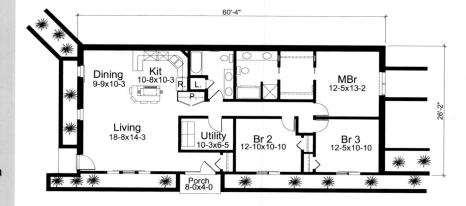

60'-4"

26'-2"

Dining
9-9x10-3

Kit
10-8x10-3

R. L.
P.

MBr
12-5x13-2

Living
18-8x14-3

Utility
10-3x6-5

Br 2
12-10x10-10

Br 3
12-5x10-10

Porch
8-0x4-0

**To order this plan, visit the Menards Building Materials Desk.**

*Stoneview*

## Cottage With Atrium

969 total square feet of living area

### Special features

- Eye-pleasing facade enjoys stone accents with country porch for quiet evenings
- A bayed dining area, cozy fireplace and atrium with sunny two-story windows are the many features of the living room
- Step-saver kitchen includes a pass-through snack bar
- 325 square feet of optional living area on the lower level
- 2 bedrooms, 1 bath, 1-car drive under rear entry garage
- Walk-out basement foundation

### Price Code AA

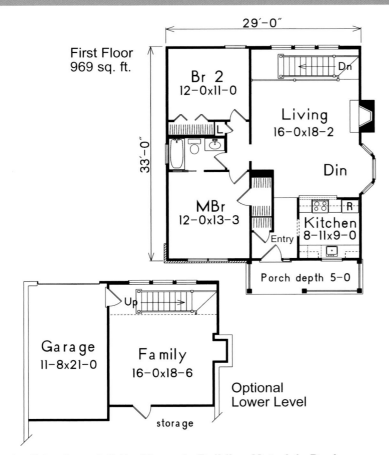

First Floor
969 sq. ft.

29'-0"

33'-0"

Br 2
12-0x11-0

Living
16-0x18-2

Din

MBr
12-0x13-3

Kitchen
8-11x9-0

Entry

Dn

Porch depth 5-0

Garage
11-8x21-0

Family
16-0x18-6

Up

Optional
Lower Level

storage

**To order this plan, visit the Menards Building Materials Desk.**

## Holland

## Great Room Window Adds Character Inside And Out

1,368 total square feet of living area

### Special features

- Entry foyer steps down to an open living area which combines the great room and formal dining area
- Vaulted master bedroom includes a box-bay window and a bath with a large vanity, separate tub and shower
- Cozy breakfast area features direct access to the patio and pass-through kitchen
- Handy linen closet is located in the hall
- 3 bedrooms, 2 baths, 2-car garage
- Basement foundation

### Price Code A

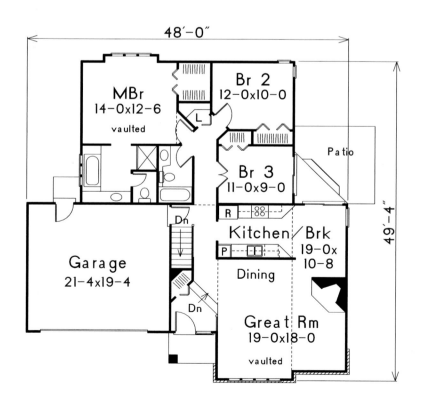

**To order this plan, visit the Menards Building Materials Desk.**

*Lauderdale*

## Divided Bedroom Areas Lend Privacy

1,833 total square feet of living area

### Special features

- Master bedroom suite comes with a garden tub, walk-in closet and bay window
- Walk-through kitchen has an organized feel and a nearby breakfast room
- Front bay windows offer a deluxe touch
- Foyer with convenient coat closet opens into large vaulted living room with an attractive fireplace
- 3 bedrooms, 2 baths, 2-car drive under garage
- Basement foundation

### Price Code C

Deck

Dining
12-6x11-6

Kit
9-0x11-6

Brk
9-8x11-6

P

Br 3
13-6x11-6

Dn

R

W
D

MBr
13-6x17-0

Living
19-8x15-6
vaulted

Foyer

Br 2
13-6x11-6

Porch

62'-0"

32'-0"

*Canton*

## Double Dormers Accent This Cozy Vacation Retreat

581 total square feet of living area

### Special features

- Kitchen/living room features space for dining and spiral steps leading to the loft area
- Large loft area can easily be converted to a bedroom or home office
- Entry space has a unique built-in display niche
- 1 bedroom, 1 bath
- Slab foundation

**Price Code AAA**

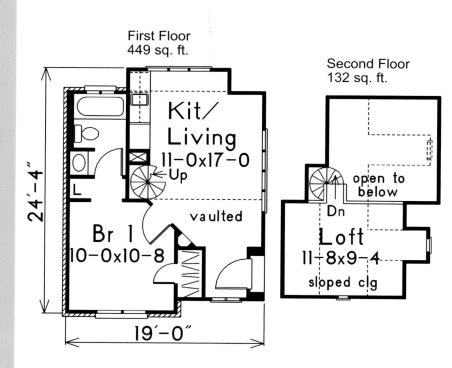

First Floor
449 sq. ft.

Second Floor
132 sq. ft.

Kit/Living
11-0x17-0
Up

vaulted

Br 1
10-0x10-8

24'-4"

19'-0"

open to below

Dn

Loft
11-8x9-4

sloped clg

*Ridgewood*

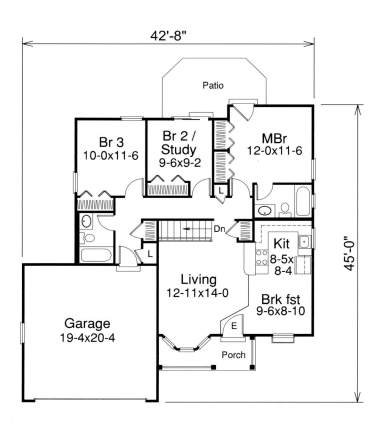

42'-8"

Patio

Br 3
10-0x11-6

Br 2 /
Study
9-6x9-2

MBr
12-0x11-6

L

Dn

L

Kit
8-5x
8-4

Living
12-11x14-0

Brk fst
9-6x8-10

Garage
19-4x20-4

E

Porch

45'-0"

## Excellent Home For A Small Family

1,062 total square feet of living area

### Special features

- Handsome appeal created by triple-gable facade
- An efficient U-shaped kitchen features a snack bar and breakfast room and is open to the living room with bay window
- Both the master bedroom, with its own private bath, and bedroom #2/study enjoy access to rear patio
- 3 bedrooms, 2 baths, 2-car garage
- Basement foundation

## Price Code AA

**MENARDS®**

*Hatteras I*

## Plenty Of Room For The Growing Family

1,705 total square feet of living area

### Special features

■ Two bedrooms on the first floor for convenience and two bedrooms on the second for privacy

■ L-shaped kitchen adjacent to dining room accesses the outdoors

■ 2" x 6" exterior walls available, please order plan #M03-001D-0110

■ 4 bedrooms, 2 baths

■ Crawl space foundation, drawings also include basement and slab foundations

### Price Code B

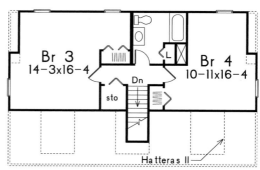

Second Floor
665 sq. ft.

Br 3
14–3x16–4

Br 4
10–11x16–4

Dn

sto

Hatteras II

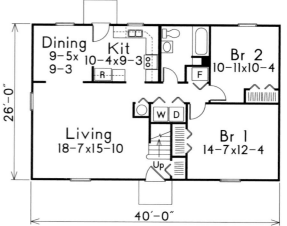

First Floor
1,040 sq. ft.

Dining
9–5x
9–3

Kit
10–4x9–3

Br 2
10–11x10–4

Living
18–7x15–10

Br 1
14–7x12–4

Up

26'–0"

40'–0"

**To order this plan, visit the Menards Building Materials Desk.**

*Beaverhill*

## Designed For Seclusion

624 total square feet of living area

### Special features

- The combination of stone, vertical siding, lots of glass and a low roof line creates a cozy retreat
- Vaulted living area features a free-standing fireplace that heats the adjacent stone wall
- Efficient kitchen includes a dining area and view onto an angular deck
- Two bedrooms share a hall bath with shower
- 2 bedrooms, 1 bath
- Pier foundation

### Price Code AAA

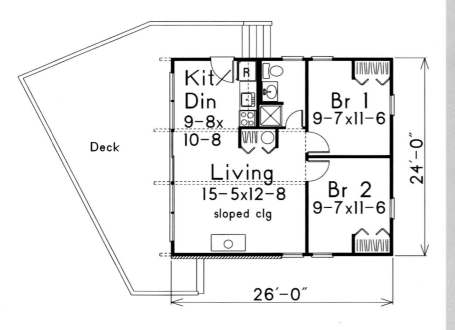

Deck

Kit
Din
9-8x
10-8

Br 1
9-7x11-6

Living
15-5x12-8
sloped clg

Br 2
9-7x11-6

24'-0"

26'-0"

**To order this plan, visit the Menards Building Materials Desk.**

*Bayshore*

# Lake House With Space For A Boat, Two Jet-Skis And A Car

**1,498 total square feet of living area**

## Special features

- A perfect home for a narrow and sloping lot featuring both front and rear garages
- Large living room has fireplace, rear outdoor balcony and a pass-through snack bar to a spacious U-shaped kitchen with adjacent dining area
- Roomy master bedroom with luxury bath and two walk-in closets
- 2 bedrooms, 2 1/2 baths, 1-car garage and a 2-car rear entry drive-under garage
- Walk-out basement foundation

**Price Code A**

22'-0"

First Floor
827 sq. ft.

Balcony

Living
21-4x14-0

Dining
10-6x9-0

Kitchen
10-4x11-8

Dn

R

47'-0"

Up

Garage
13-0x20-4

Entry

Porch

MBr
17-0x12-0

D
W
L

Seat

Dn

Balcony

Br 2
13-0x14-9

Second Floor
671 sq. ft.

**To order this plan, visit the Menards Building Materials Desk.**

**MENARDS** ®

*Addlebury*

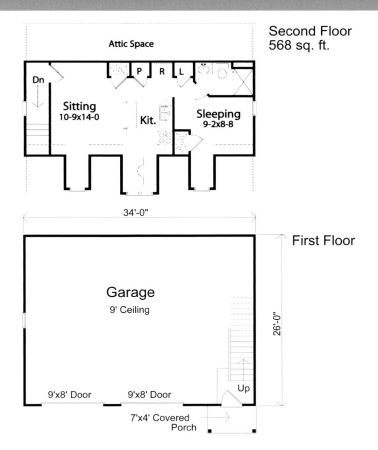

Second Floor
568 sq. ft.

Attic Space

Dn

Sitting
10-9x14-0

P R L

Kit.

Sleeping
9-2x8-8

First Floor

34'-0"

Garage
9' Ceiling

26'-0"

9'x8' Door    9'x8' Door    Up

7'x4' Covered
Porch

## 2-Car Garage Apartment

568 total square feet of living area

### Special features

- A covered entry welcomes guests into this delightful garage apartment
- Beautiful dormers brighten the interior
- The kitchen counter overlooks the sitting area for efficiency
- 1 bedroom, 1 bath, 2-car garage
- Basement foundation

### Price Code AAA

**To order this plan, visit the Menards Building Materials Desk.**

175

*Foreston*

## Cozy Ranch Home

950 total square feet of living area

### Special features

- Deck is attached to the kitchen, perfect for outdoor dining
- Vaulted ceiling, open stairway and fireplace complement the great room
- Bedroom #2 with a sloped ceiling and box-bay window can convert to a den
- Master bedroom has a walk-in closet, plant shelf, separate dressing area and private access to bath
- Kitchen has garage access and opens to the great room
- 2 bedrooms, 1 bath, 1-car garage
- Basement foundation

### Price Code AA

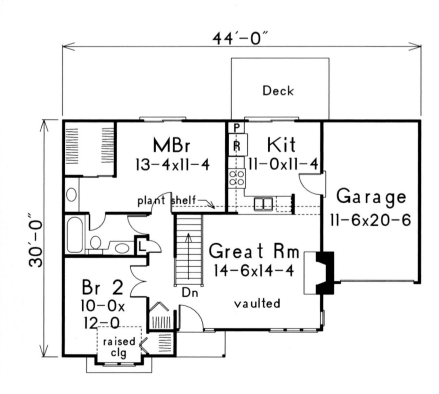

**To order this plan, visit the Menards Building Materials Desk.**

*Geneva*

## A Chalet For Lakeside Living

1,280 total square feet of living area

### Special features

- Attention to architectural detail has created the look of an authentic Swiss cottage
- Spacious living room, adjacent kitchenette and dining area all enjoy views to the front deck
- Hall bath shared by two sizable bedrooms is included on the first and second floors
- 4 bedrooms, 2 baths
- Crawl space foundation, drawings also include basement foundation

### Price Code A

**28'-0"**

**32'-0"**

Br 1
10-1x8-11

Br 2
10-1x11-4

Kit
8-9x
10-1

R

F
W
D

Up

Dining
10-4x10-11

Living
14-11x13-4

Deck

**First Floor**
832 sq. ft.

Br 3
13-5x10-3

sloped clg

Dn

L

Br 4
13-5x10-1

Balcony

**Second Floor**
448 sq. ft.

*Chestnut*

# Gable Facade Adds Appeal To This Ranch

1,304 total square feet of living area

## Special features

- Covered entrance leads into the family room with a cozy fireplace
- 10' ceilings in kitchen, dining and family rooms
- Master bedroom features a coffered ceiling, walk-in closet and private bath
- Efficient kitchen includes large window over the sink
- 3 bedrooms, 2 baths, 2-car garage
- Slab foundation

## Price Code A

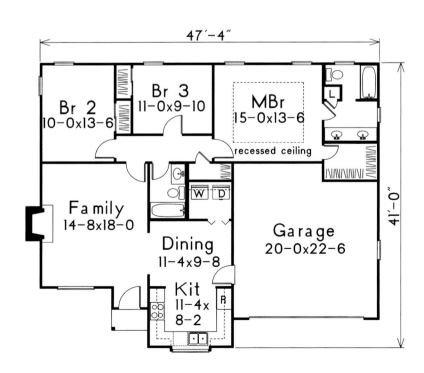

47'-4"

41'-0"

Br 2
10-0x13-6

Br 3
11-0x9-10

MBr
15-0x13-6
recessed ceiling

W  D

Family
14-8x18-0

Dining
11-4x9-8

Kit
11-4x
8-2

Garage
20-0x22-6

To order this plan, visit the Menards Building Materials Desk.

*Roseport*

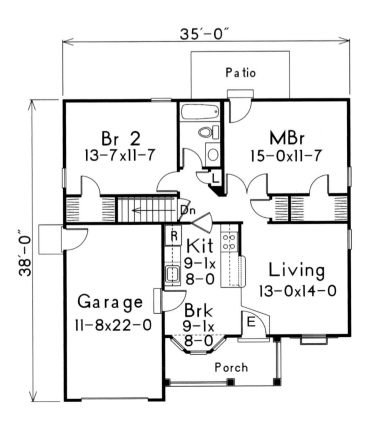

## Elegance In A Starter Or Retirement Home

888 total square feet of living area

### Special features

- Home features an eye-catching exterior and has a spacious porch
- The breakfast room with bay window is open to the living room and adjoins the kitchen with pass-through snack bar
- The bedrooms are quite roomy and feature walk-in closets
- The master bedroom has a double-door entry and access to the rear patio
- 2 bedrooms, 1 bath, 1-car garage
- Basement foundation

### Price Code AAA

*Foxrun*

## Contemporary Escape

1,836 total square feet of living area

### Special features

- Foyer sparkles with spiral stair, a sloped ceiling and celestial windows
- Living room enjoys fireplace with bookshelves and view to the outdoors
- U-shaped kitchen includes eat-in breakfast area and dining nearby
- Master bedroom revels in having a balcony overlooking the living room, a large walk-in closet and private bath
- 3 bedrooms, 2 1/2 baths
- Crawl space foundation, drawings also include slab foundation

### Price Code C

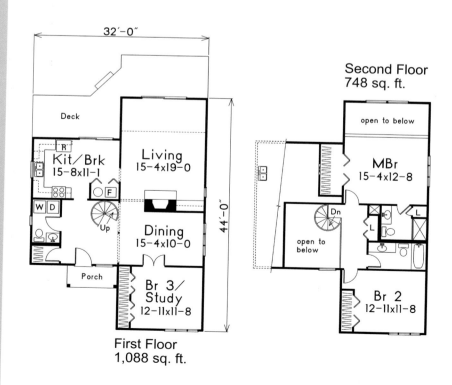

Second Floor
748 sq. ft.

First Floor
1,088 sq. ft.

**To order this plan, visit the Menards Building Materials Desk.**

*Dunbar*

Second Floor
868 sq. ft.

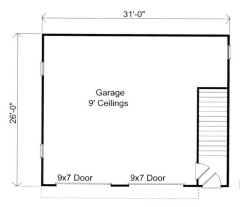

First Floor

## 2-Car Garage Apartment

868 total square feet of living area

### Special features

- Large utility room adds convenience to this garage apartment
- The dining and great rooms flow together
- The kitchen features a snack bar counter
- 1 bedroom, 1 bath, 2-car garage
- Basement foundation

## Price Code AAA

**To order this plan, visit the Menards Building Materials Desk.**

*Hatteras II*

## Front Dormers Add Light And Space

1,705 total square feet of living area

### Special features

- Cozy design includes two bedrooms on the first floor and two bedrooms on the second floor for added privacy
- L-shaped kitchen provides easy access to the dining room and the outdoors
- Convenient first floor laundry area
- 2" x 6" exterior walls available, please order plan #M03-001D-0111
- 4 bedrooms, 2 baths
- Crawl space foundation, drawings also include basement and slab foundations

### Price Code B

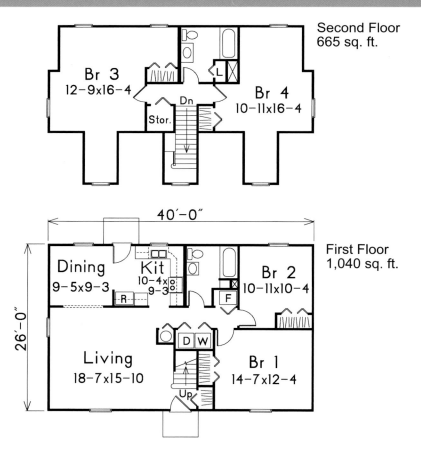

Second Floor
665 sq. ft.

Br 3
12-9x16-4

Br 4
10-11x16-4

Dn

Stor.

L

40'-0"

First Floor
1,040 sq. ft.

Dining
9-5x9-3

Kit
10-4x
9-3

Br 2
10-11x10-4

R

F

26'-0"

Living
18-7x15-10

D W

Br 1
14-7x12-4

Up

**To order this plan, visit the Menards Building Materials Desk.**

**MENARDS**®

*Trailbridge*

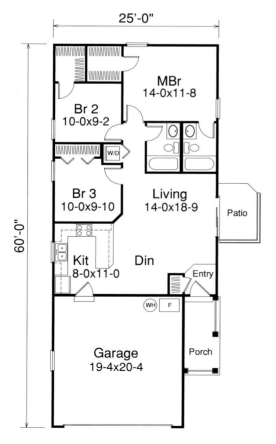

25'-0"

60'-0"

MBr
14-0x11-8

Br 2
10-0x9-2

W/D

Br 3
10-0x9-10

Living
14-0x18-9

Patio

Kit
8-0x11-0

Din

Entry

WH   F

Garage
19-4x20-4

Porch

## Ideal Design For A Narrow Lot

983 total square feet of living area

### Special features

- Spacious front porch leads you into the living and dining areas open to a pass-through kitchen
- A small patio with privacy fence creates exterior access from the living room
- The master bedroom includes a large walk-in closet and its own private full bath
- 3 bedrooms, 2 baths, 2-car garage
- Crawl space foundation, drawings also include slab foundation

### Price Code AA

**To order this plan, visit the Menards Building Materials Desk.**

**MENARDS**®

*Conifer*

## Vacation Retreat With Attractive A-Frame Styling

1,312 total square feet of living area

### Special features

- Expansive deck extends directly off living area
- L-shaped kitchen is organized and efficient
- Bedroom to the left of the kitchen makes a great quiet retreat or office
- Living area is flanked with windows for light
- 3 bedrooms, 1 bath
- Pier foundation

### Price Code A

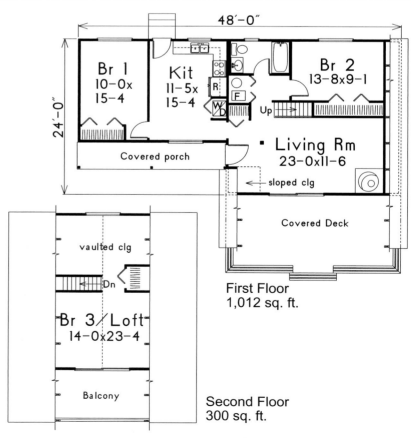

First Floor
1,012 sq. ft.

Second Floor
300 sq. ft.

**To order this plan, visit the Menards Building Materials Desk.**

*Brixworth*

Second Floor
570 sq. ft.

First Floor
1,104 sq. ft.

## Ideal Two-Story For A Narrow Lot

1,674 total square feet of living area

### Special features

- Energy efficient home with 2" x 6" exterior walls
- Covered entrance opens to find open living and dining rooms that are designed for entertaining
- A quiet study could also be used as a guest bedroom
- The master bedroom is secluded on the first floor while two additional bedrooms share the second floor
- 3 bedrooms, 2 baths
- Basement foundation

### Price Code B

**To order this plan, visit the Menards Building Materials Desk.**

*Fernwood*

## Vaulted Living Area With Corner Fireplace

1,448 total square feet of living area

### Special features

- Dining room conveniently adjoins kitchen and accesses rear deck
- Private first floor master bedroom
- Secondary bedrooms share a bath and cozy loft area
- 3 bedrooms, 2 1/2 baths, 2-car garage
- Basement foundation

### Price Code A

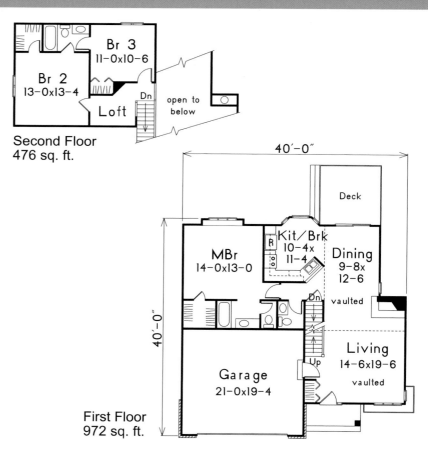

Second Floor
476 sq. ft.

First Floor
972 sq. ft.

To order this plan, visit the Menards Building Materials Desk.

*Shadyhill*

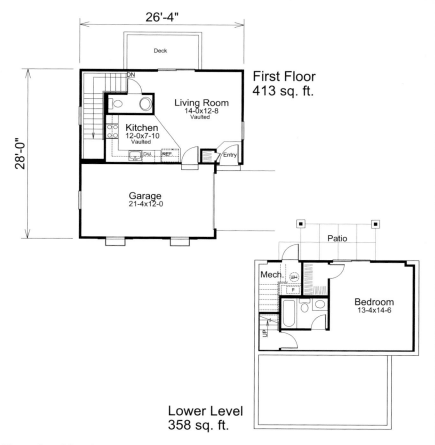

26'-4"

Deck

DN

Living Room
14-0x12-8
Vaulted

Kitchen
12-0x7-10
Vaulted

D.W.  REF.

Entry

Garage
21-4x12-0

28'-0"

**First Floor**
**413 sq. ft.**

Patio

Mech.

UH

F

UP

Bedroom
13-4x14-6

**Lower Level**
**358 sq. ft.**

## Little Cottage With Big Spaces

771 total square feet of living area

### Special features

- The living room includes a vaulted ceiling, separate entry with guest closet and glass doors to the rear deck
- A vaulted ceiling and overhead plant shelf are two attractive features of the L-shaped kitchen
- The lower floor is comprised of a spacious bedroom complete with a private bath, walk-in closet and glass doors to the rear patio
- 1 bedroom, 1 1/2 baths, 1-car side entry garage
- Walk-out basement foundation

## Price Code AAA

**To order this plan, visit the Menards Building Materials Desk.**

*Cochise*

## A Vacation Oasis

1,106 total square feet of living area

### Special features

- Delightful A-frame provides exciting vacation-style living all year long
- Deck accesses a large living room with an open soaring ceiling
- Enormous sleeping area is provided on the second floor with balcony overlook to living room below
- 2 bedrooms, 1 bath
- Pier foundation

### Price Code AA

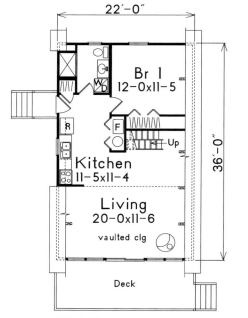

First Floor
792 sq. ft.

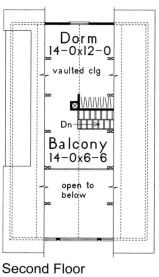

Second Floor
314 sq. ft.

**To order this plan, visit the Menards Building Materials Desk.**

**MENARDS**®

*Westridge*

## Convenient Center Entry

1,134 total square feet of living area

### Special features

- Kitchen has plenty of counterspace, an island worktop, large pantry and access to the garage
- Living room features a vaulted ceiling, fireplace and access to an expansive patio
- Bedroom #1 has a large walk-in closet
- Convenient linen closet in the hall
- 2 bedrooms, 1 bath, 2-car garage
- Basement foundation

### Price Code AA

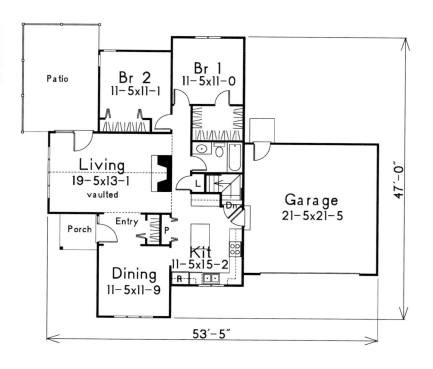

*Chickadance*

## Covered Porch Highlights This Home

1,364 total square feet of living area

### Special features

- Bedrooms are separated from the living area for privacy
- Master bedroom has a private bath and large walk-in closet
- Laundry area is conveniently located near the kitchen
- Bright and spacious great room
- Built-in pantry in the kitchen
- 3 bedrooms, 2 baths, optional 2-car garage
- Basement foundation

### Price Code A

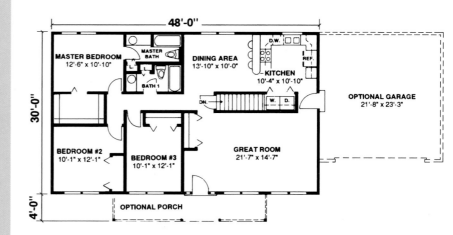

To order this plan, visit the Menards Building Materials Desk.

*Pinewood*

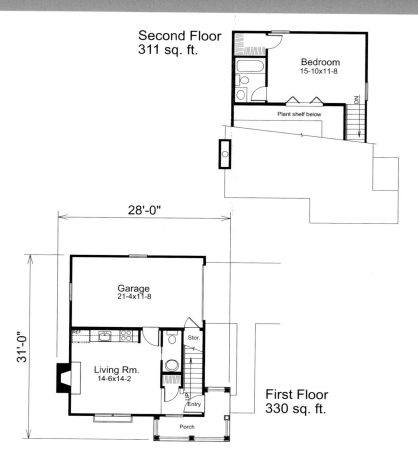

Second Floor
311 sq. ft.

Bedroom
15-10x11-8

Plant shelf below

DN

28'-0"

31'-0"

Garage
21-4x11-8

REF.

Stor.

Living Rm.
14-6x14-2

UP

Entry

Porch

First Floor
330 sq. ft.

## Perfect For A Cottage Retreat

641 total square feet of living area

### Special features

- Charming exterior enjoys a wrap-around porch and a large feature window with arch and planter box
- The living room features a kitchenette, fireplace, vaulted ceiling with plant shelf, separate entry with coat closet and access to adjacent powder room and garage
- The stair leads to a spacious second floor bedroom complete with bath, walk-in closet and a unique opening with louvered doors for an overview of the living room below
- 1 bedroom, 1 1/2 baths, 1-car side entry garage
- Slab foundation

### Price Code AAA

**To order this plan, visit the Menards Building Materials Desk.**

*Westerry*

## Answer To A Tapered Lot

986 total square feet of living area

### Special features

- Wide and tall windows in the kitchen, dining and living areas create bright and cheerful spaces
- Three bedrooms with plenty of closet space and an oversized hall bath are located at the rear of the home
- An extra-deep garage has storage space at the rear and access to the patio behind the garage
- Convenient linen closet is located in the hall
- 3 bedrooms, 1 bath, 1-car garage
- Basement foundation, drawings also include crawl space and slab foundations

### Price Code AA

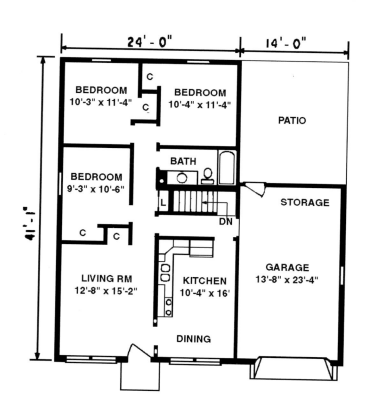

**To order this plan, visit the Menards Building Materials Desk.**

*Vicksdale*

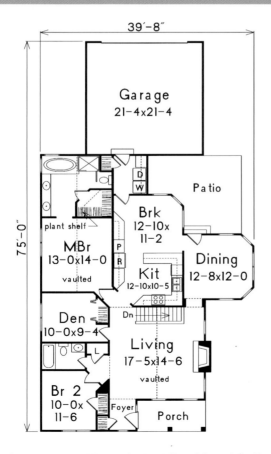

## Innovative Design For That Narrow Lot

1,558 total square feet of living area

### Special features

- Illuminated spaces are created by visual access to the outdoor living areas
- Vaulted master bedroom features a private bath with whirlpool tub, separate shower and large walk-in closet
- Convenient laundry area has garage access
- Practical den or third bedroom is perfect for a variety of uses
- U-shaped kitchen is adjacent to the sunny breakfast area
- 2 bedrooms, 2 baths, 2-car rear entry garage
- Basement foundation

### Price Code B

**To order this plan, visit the Menards Building Materials Desk.**

*Stonehaven*

## Earth Berm Home With Style

1,480 total square feet of living area

### Special features

- Home has great looks and lots of space
- Nestled in a hillside with only one exposed exterior wall, this home offers efficiency, protection and affordability
- Triple patio doors with an arched transom bathe the living room with sunlight
- The kitchen features a snack bar open to the living room, large built-in pantry and adjoins a spacious dining area
- 2 bedrooms, 2 baths, 2-car garage
- Slab foundation

### Price Code A

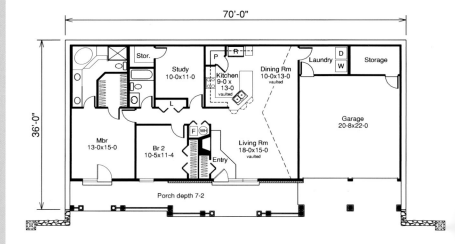

**To order this plan, visit the Menards Building Materials Desk.**

*Oakwood*

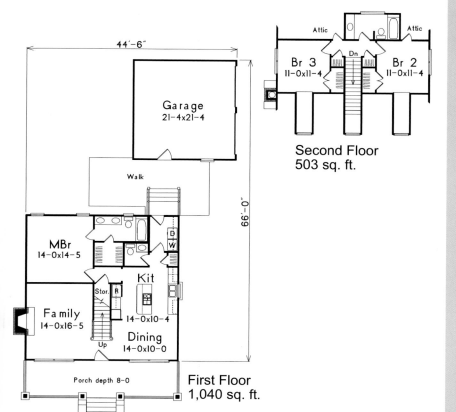

## Relax On The Covered Front Porch

1,543 total square feet of living area

### Special features

- Fireplace serves as the focal point of the large family room
- Efficient floor plan keeps hallways at a minimum
- Laundry room connects the kitchen to the garage
- Private first floor master bedroom has a walk-in closet and bath
- 3 bedrooms, 2 1/2 baths, 2-car detached side entry garage
- Slab foundation, drawings also include crawl space foundation

### Price Code B

**Garage**
21-4x21-4

**Walk**

Attic — **Br 3** 11-0x11-4 — **Dn** — **Br 2** 11-0x11-4 — Attic

Second Floor
503 sq. ft.

44'-6"

66'-0"

**MBr**
14-0x14-5

**Kit**
14-0x10-4

**Family**
14-0x16-5

Stor. R

Up

**Dining**
14-0x10-0

Porch depth 8-0

First Floor
1,040 sq. ft.

**To order this plan, visit the Menards Building Materials Desk.**

*Farmview*

## Two-Story Foyer Adds Spacious Feeling

1,833 total square feet of living area

### Special features

- Large master bedroom includes a spacious bath with garden tub, separate shower and large walk-in closet
- The spacious dining area is brightened by large windows and patio access
- Detached two-car garage with walkway leading to house adds charm to this country home
- 3 bedrooms, 2 1/2 baths, 2-car detached side entry garage
- Crawl space foundation, drawings also include slab foundation

### Price Code D

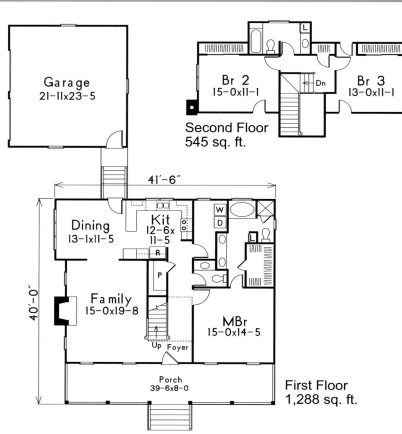

Garage
21-11x23-5

Br 2
15-0x11-1

Br 3
13-0x11-1

Second Floor
545 sq. ft.

41'-6"

Dining
13-1x11-5

Kit
12-6x11-5

40'-0"

Family
15-0x19-8

MBr
15-0x14-5

Up  Foyer

Porch
39-6x8-0

First Floor
1,288 sq. ft.

**To order this plan, visit the Menards Building Materials Desk.**

*Galena*

## Roughing It In Luxury

1,200 total square feet of living area

### Special features

- Ornate ranch-style railing enhances exterior while the stone fireplace provides a visual anchor
- Spectacular living room features an inviting fireplace and adjoins a charming kitchen with dining area
- Two second floor bedrooms share a full bath
- 3 bedrooms, 1 1/2 baths
- Crawl space foundation, drawings also include slab foundation

## Price Code A

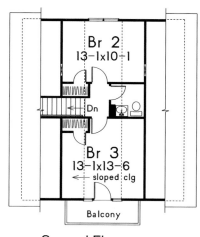

26'-0"

30'-0"

Br 1
9-4x12-6

Kit
10-1x
9-5

Up

Living
25-4x13-2

Deck

First Floor
780 sq. ft.

Br 2
13-1x10-1

Dn

Br 3
13-1x13-6
← sloped clg

Balcony

Second Floor
420 sq. ft.

*Stonetrail*

# Apartment Garage Plus RV Storage

713 total square feet of living area

## Special features

- An attractive exterior has been created with the use of arches, stonework and a roof dormer
- The living room features a dining area with bay window and a separate entry with access to garage and stair to second floor
- A very efficient and well-equipped L-shaped kitchen has view to the rear yard and a built-in pantry
- The second floor offers a large bedroom with alcove for a desk, walk-in closet and a private bath off the hall
- 1 bedroom, 1 1/2 bath, 2-car garage, RV garage
- Slab foundation

## Price Code AAA

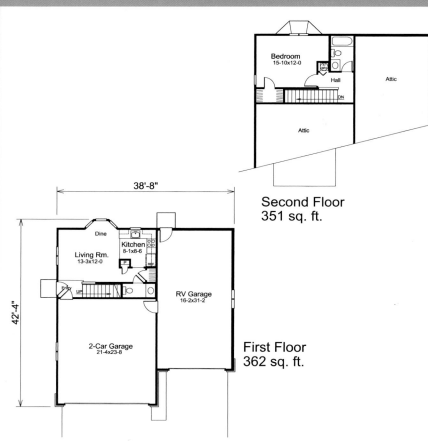

Second Floor
351 sq. ft.

First Floor
362 sq. ft.

**To order this plan, visit the Menards Building Materials Desk.**

*Provider 1*

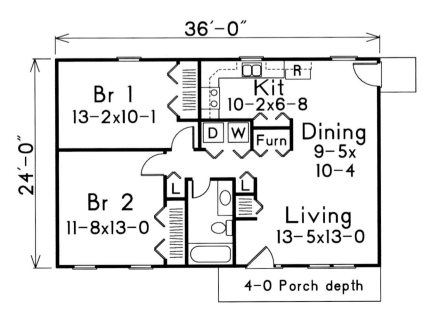

36'-0"

24'-0"

Br 1
13-2x10-1

Kit
10-2x6-8

R

D W Furn

Dining
9-5x
10-4

Br 2
11-8x13-0

L

L

Living
13-5x13-0

4-0 Porch depth

## Perfect Home For A Small Family

864 total square feet of living area

### Special features

- L-shaped kitchen with convenient pantry is adjacent to dining area
- Easy access to laundry area, linen closet and storage closet
- Both bedrooms include ample closet space
- 2 bedrooms, 1 bath
- Crawl space foundation, drawings also include basement and slab foundations

### Price Code AAA

*Zurich*

## Cozy Cottage Living

1,280 total square feet of living area

### Special features

- A front porch deck, ornate porch roof, massive stone fireplace and Old-English windows all generate an inviting appearance
- The large living room accesses the kitchen and spacious dining area
- Two spacious bedrooms with ample closet space comprise the second floor
- 4 bedrooms, 2 baths
- Basement foundation, drawings also include slab and crawl space foundations

**Price Code A**

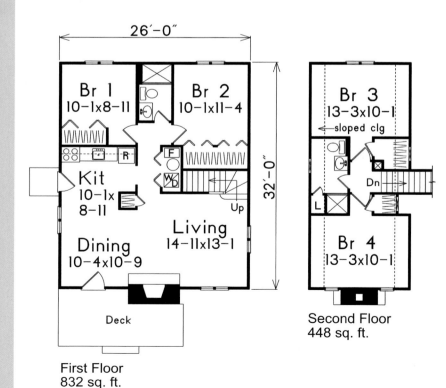

26'-0"

32'-0"

Br 1
10-1x8-11

Br 2
10-1x11-4

Kit
10-1x
8-11

Living
14-11x13-1

Dining
10-4x10-9

Up

Deck

**First Floor**
832 sq. ft.

Br 3
13-3x10-1
sloped clg

Dn

Br 4
13-3x10-1

L

**Second Floor**
448 sq. ft.

**To order this plan, visit the Menards Building Materials Desk.**

*Delta Queen 11*

## Layout Creates Large Open Living Area

1,285 total square feet of living area

### Special features

- Large storage area on back of home
- Master bedroom includes dressing area, private bath and built-in bookcase
- Kitchen features pantry, breakfast bar and complete view to dining room
- 2" x 6" exterior walls available, please order plan #M03-001D-0120
- 3 bedrooms, 2 baths
- Crawl space foundation, drawings also include basement and slab foundations

**Price Code B**

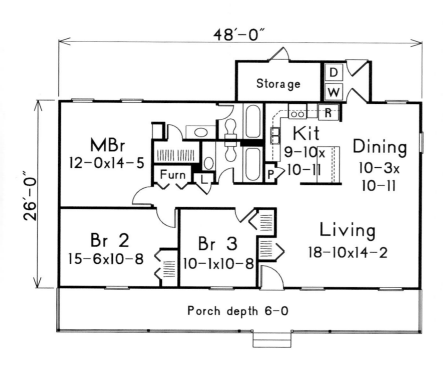

48'-0"

26'-0"

Storage

D
W

Kit
9-10x
10-11

Dining
10-3x
10-11

MBr
12-0x14-5

Furn

P

Br 2
15-6x10-8

Br 3
10-1x10-8

Living
18-10x14-2

Porch depth 6-0

## La Demeure

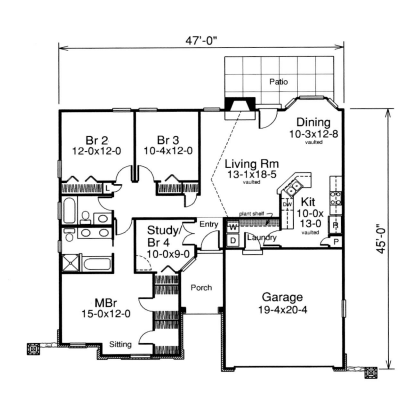

## French Country Style For A Narrow Lot

1,519 total square feet of living area

### Special features

- The large living room boasts a vaulted ceiling with plant shelf, fireplace, and opens to the bayed dining area
- The kitchen has an adjoining laundry/mud room and features a vaulted ceiling, snack counter open to the living and dining areas and a built-in pantry
- Two walk-in closets, a stylish bath and small sitting area accompany the master bedroom
- 4 bedrooms, 2 baths, 2-car garage
- Crawl space foundation, drawings also include slab and basement foundations

### Price Code B

**To order this plan, visit the Menards Building Materials Desk.**

*Oakberry*

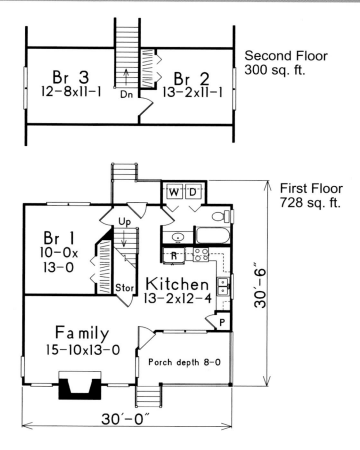

Second Floor
300 sq. ft.

Br 3
12-8x11-1

Dn

Br 2
13-2x11-1

First Floor
728 sq. ft.

W  D

Up

Br 1
10-0x
13-0

Stor

Kitchen
13-2x12-4

R

P

30'-6"

Family
15-10x13-0

Porch depth 8-0

30'-0"

## Quaint Country Home Is Ideal

1,028 total square feet of living area

### Special features

- Well-designed bath contains laundry facilities
- L-shaped kitchen has a handy pantry
- Tall windows flank family room fireplace
- Cozy covered porch provides unique angled entry into home
- 3 bedrooms, 1 bath
- Crawl space foundation

### Price Code AA

*Timberland*

## Compact Ranch Is An Ideal Starter Home

988 total square feet of living area

### Special features

- Great room features a corner fireplace
- Vaulted ceiling and corner windows add space and light in great room
- Eat-in kitchen with vaulted ceiling accesses deck for outdoor living
- Master bedroom features separate vanities and private access to the bath
- 2 bedrooms, 1 bath, 2-car garage
- Basement foundation

### Price Code AA

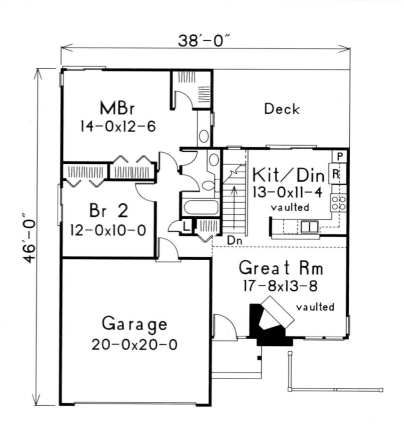

38'-0"

46'-0"

MBr
14-0x12-6

Deck

Br 2
12-0x10-0

Kit/Din
13-0x11-4
vaulted

Dn

Great Rm
17-8x13-8
vaulted

Garage
20-0x20-0

**To order this plan, visit the Menards Building Materials Desk.**

# Plan #M03-008D-0156

**MENARDS**®

Rear View

*Amberhill*

## Trendsetting Contemporary Retreat

1,528 total square feet of living area

### Special features

- Large deck complements handsome exterior
- Family room provides a welcome space for family get-togethers and includes a sloped ceiling and access to the studio and sleeping loft
- Kitchen features dining space and a view to the deck
- A hall bath is shared by two bedrooms on the first floor which have ample closet space
- 2 bedrooms, 1 bath
- Crawl space foundation

## Price Code B

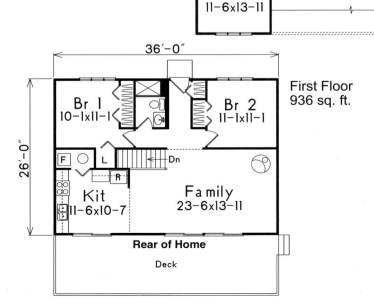

Second Floor
592 sq. ft.

Sleeping Loft
35-4x11-5

Dn

open to below

Studio
11-6x13-11

First Floor
936 sq. ft.

36'-0"

26'-0"

Br 1
10-1x11-1

Br 2
11-1x11-1

F  L  Dn

Kit
11-6x10-7

Family
23-6x13-11

Rear of Home

Deck

**To order this plan, visit the Menards Building Materials Desk.**

205

*Kenrick*

## Corner Windows
## Grace Library

1,824 total square feet of living area

### Special features

- Living room features a 10' ceiling, fireplace and media center
- Dining room includes a bay window and convenient kitchen access
- Master bedroom features a large walk-in closet and luxurious bath with a double-door entry
- Modified U-shaped kitchen features pantry and bar
- 3 bedrooms, 2 baths, 2-car detached garage
- Slab foundation

### Price Code C

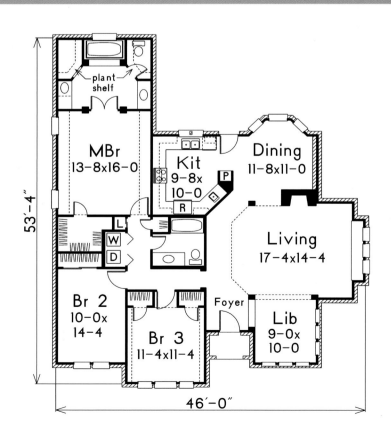

**To order this plan, visit the Menards Building Materials Desk.**

*Newton Park*

## Studio Apartment Garage With Office

656 total square feet of living area

### Special features

- Simple but cleverly designed exterior disguises this two-story structure as a one-story
- Located behind the garage is the perfect room for an office or workshop and has glass sliding doors to a rear patio
- The front entrance leads to an entry that accesses both the garage and apartment
- A well-equipped kitchenette, full bath and a closet/mechanical room are the featured spaces of the efficient studio apartment
- Studio room, 1 bath, 1-car garage
- Slab foundation

### Price Code AAA

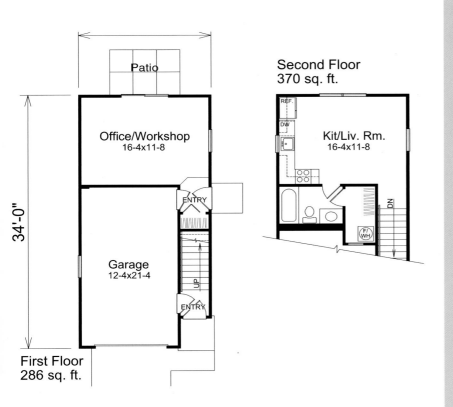

Patio

Office/Workshop
16-4x11-8

ENTRY

Garage
12-4x21-4

UP

ENTRY

34'-0"

First Floor
286 sq. ft.

Second Floor
370 sq. ft.

REF.

DW

Kit/Liv. Rm.
16-4x11-8

DN

F/WH

*Northland*

## Perfect Fit For A Narrow Site

1,270 total square feet of living area

### Special features

- Spacious living area features angled stairs, vaulted ceiling, exciting fireplace and deck access
- Master bedroom includes a walk-in closet and private bath
- Dining and living rooms join to create an open atmosphere
- Eat-in kitchen has a convenient pass-through to the dining room
- 3 bedrooms, 2 baths, 2-car garage
- Basement foundation

### Price Code A

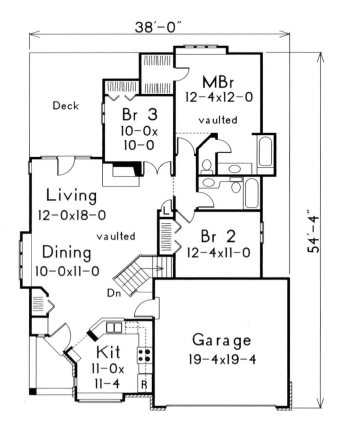

**To order this plan, visit the Menards Building Materials Desk.**

*Yukon*

## First Floor
21'-0"

Stor · Deck

Kit
10-4x
9-2

R

Up · ladder

Living
20-4x11-8

24'-0"

Deck

**First Floor**
495 sq. ft.

## Second Floor

Br 1
14-0x9-2

Dn · ladder

Br 2
14-0x11-4

Deck

**Second Floor**
370 sq. ft.

## Terrific Design Loaded With Extras

865 total square feet of living area

### Special features

- Central living area provides an enormous amount of space for gathering around the fireplace
- The outdoor ladder on the wrap-around deck connects the top deck with the main deck
- Kitchen is bright and cheerful with lots of windows and access to the deck
- 2 bedrooms, 1 bath
- Pier foundation

**Price Code AAA**

**To order this plan, visit the Menards Building Materials Desk.**

*Autumn Lakes*

## Country Home For A Sloping Lot

1,148 total square feet of living area

### Special features

- The large wrap-around porch is ideal for an early morning breakfast or for a late evening lounging
- A separate entry, full masonry fireplace and balcony/dining area that overlooks the two-story atrium with floor-to-ceiling window wall are some of the many amenities of the vaulted great room
- The spacious kitchen features an angled snack bar and enjoys easy access to the laundry and garage
- The atrium is open to 462 square feet of optional living area below
- 2 bedrooms, 1 bath, 1-car side entry garage
- Walk-out basement foundation

### Price Code AA

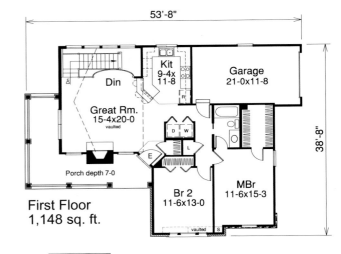

53'-8"

38'-8"

Kit 9-4x 11-8

Din

Garage 21-0x11-8

Great Rm. 15-4x20-0 vaulted

D W

L

E

Porch depth 7-0

Br 2 11-6x13-0

MBr 11-6x15-3

**First Floor 1,148 sq. ft.**

vaulted

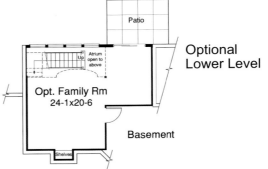

Patio

Atrium open to above

Up

**Optional Lower Level**

Opt. Family Rm 24-1x20-6

Basement

Shelves

**To order this plan, visit the Menards Building Materials Desk.**

*Greenridge*

## Convenient Ranch

1,120 total square feet of living area

### Special features

- Master bedroom includes a half bath with laundry area, linen closet and kitchen access
- Kitchen has charming double-door entry, breakfast bar and a convenient walk-in pantry
- Welcoming front porch opens to a large living room with coat closet
- 3 bedrooms, 1 1/2 baths
- Crawl space foundation, drawings also include basement and slab foundations

### Price Code AA

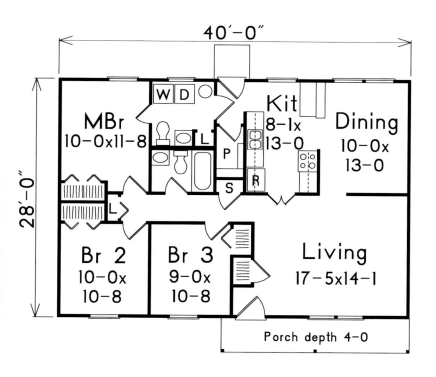

40'-0"

28'-0"

W  D

MBr
10-0x11-8

Kit
8-1x
13-0

Dining
10-0x
13-0

P

L

S

R

Br 2
10-0x
10-8

Br 3
9-0x
10-8

Living
17-5x14-1

Porch depth 4-0

**To order this plan, visit the Menards Building Materials Desk.**

*Hickory*

## Country-Style Porch Adds Charm

1,619 total square feet of living area

### Special features

- Private second floor bedroom and bath
- Kitchen features a snack bar and adjacent dining area
- Master bedroom has a private bath
- Centrally located washer and dryer
- 3 bedrooms, 3 baths
- Basement foundation, drawings also include crawl space and slab foundations

### Price Code B

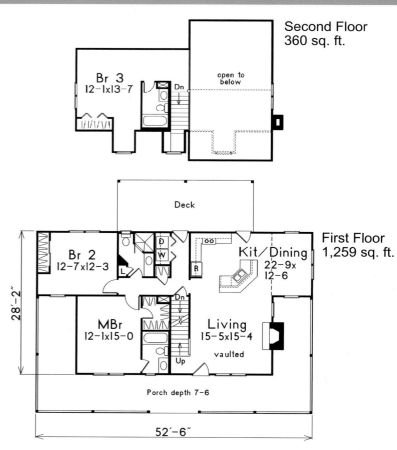

Second Floor
360 sq. ft.

Br 3
12-1x13-7

open to below

Dn

Deck

First Floor
1,259 sq. ft.

Br 2
12-7x12-3

Kit/Dining
22-9x
12-6

MBr
12-1x15-0

Living
15-5x15-4
vaulted

Dn

Up

28'-2"

Porch depth 7-6

52'-6"

**To order this plan, visit the Menards Building Materials Desk.**

*Valleyview*

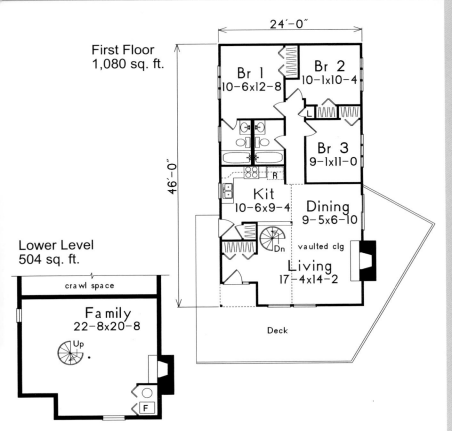

First Floor
1,080 sq. ft.

24'-0"

46'-0"

Br 1
10-6x12-8

Br 2
10-1x10-4

Br 3
9-1x11-0

Kit
10-6x9-4

Dining
9-5x6-10

vaulted clg

Living
17-4x14-2

Dn

Deck

Lower Level
504 sq. ft.

crawl space

Family
22-8x20-8

Up

F

## Nestled Oasis Romances The Sun

1,584 total square feet of living area

### Special features

- Vaulted living and dining rooms feature a stone fireplace, ascending spiral staircase and a separate vestibule with guest closet
- Space-saving kitchen has an eat-in area and access to the deck
- Bedroom #1 has private access to a full bath
- 3 bedrooms, 2 baths
- Partial basement/crawl space foundation, drawings also include crawl space foundation

**Price Code B**

**To order this plan, visit the Menards Building Materials Desk.**

213

## El Gorge

# Cleverly Angled Walls Add Interest To Home

1,400 total square feet of living area

## Special features

- Inside and out, this home is pleasingly different
- Activity area showcases large free-standing fireplace and spacious dining area with views
- Laundry area is provided in a very functional kitchen
- Master bedroom with a double-door entry is a grand bedroom with nice amenities
- 2 bedrooms, 2 baths
- Crawl space foundation

## Price Code A

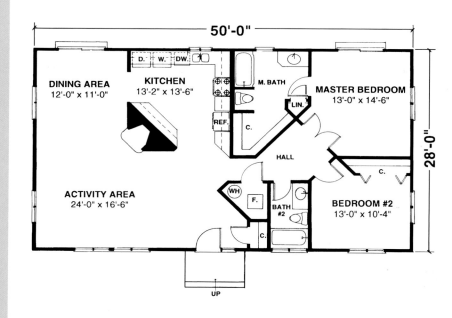

**To order this plan, visit the Menards Building Materials Desk.**

*Greenbay*

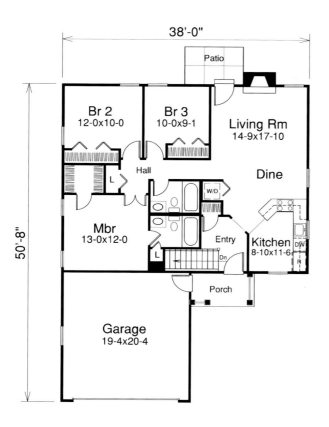

38'-0"

Patio

Br 2
12-0x10-0

Br 3
10-0x9-1

Living Rm
14-9x17-10

Hall

L

Dine

W/D

Mbr
13-0x12-0

Entry

Kitchen
8-10x11-6

DW

R

L

Dn

50'-8"

Porch

Garage
19-4x20-4

## Charming Three-Bedroom Home

1,140 total square feet of living area

### Special features

- Delightful appearance with a protective porch
- The entry, with convenient stairs to the basement, leads to spacious living and dining rooms open to the adjacent kitchen
- The master bedroom enjoys a double-door entry, walk-in closet and a private bath with its own linen closet
- 3 bedrooms, 2 baths, 2-car garage
- Basement foundation, drawings also include slab and crawl space foundations

### Price Code AA

Outdoor faucets mounted on the side of a house can freeze in cold weather, causing pipes to burst. Be sure to drain them before the first freeze. To do this, shut off the water supply leading to the faucet, then open the faucet to drain off any remaining water trapped between the faucet and the shut-off valve. An alternative to this seasonal chore: have a freeze-proof spigot installed.

*Yakutat*

# An A-Frame For Every Environment

## 618 total square feet of living area

### Special features

- Memorable family events are certain to be enjoyed on this fabulous partially covered deck
- Equally impressive is the living area with its cathedral ceiling and exposed rafters
- A kitchenette, bedroom and bath conclude the first floor with a delightful sleeping loft on the second floor
- 1 bedroom, 1 bath
- Pier foundation

### Price Code AAA

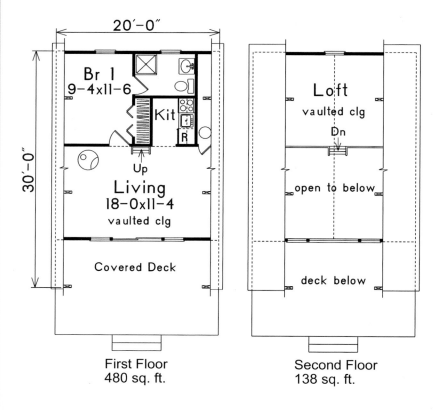

First Floor
480 sq. ft.

Second Floor
138 sq. ft.

**To order this plan, visit the Menards Building Materials Desk.**

**MENARDS**®

*Manchester*

## Country Style With Spacious Rooms

1,197 total square feet of living area

### Special features

- U-shaped kitchen includes ample workspace, breakfast bar, laundry area and direct access to the outdoors
- Large living room has a convenient coat closet
- Bedroom #1 features a large walk-in closet
- 2" x 6" exterior walls available, please order plan #M03-001D-0102
- 3 bedrooms, 1 bath
- Crawl space foundation, drawings also include basement and slab foundations

### Price Code AA

46'-0"

28'-0"

**Br 1** 13-0x12-1

D
W
F
L

**Dining** 10-2x11-0

**Kit** 10-3x11-0
R

**Br 2** 12-3x12-7

**Br 3** 10-2x12-7

**Living** 20-0x12-1

Porch depth 4-0

**To order this plan, visit the Menards Building Materials Desk.**

*Summerhouse*

## A Porch Lover's Dream Home

1,646 total square feet of living area

### Special features

- Attractive cottage features two large porch areas
- The great room includes a corner fireplace and beautiful views provided by ten windows and doors
- A U-shaped kitchen with snack counter is open to the breakfast room and enjoys access to both the side and rear porch
- The master bedroom has a luxury bath with corner tub, double vanities with makeup counter and a huge walk-in closet
- 2 bedrooms, 2 baths, 2-car side entry garage
- Basement foundation, drawings also include slab and crawl space foundations

**Price Code B**

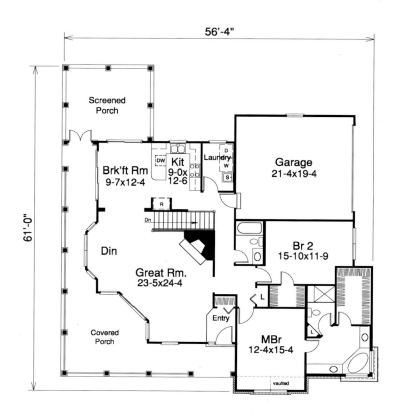

56'-4"

61'-0"

Screened Porch

Brk'ft Rm 9-7x12-4

DW

Kit 9-0x 12-6

Laundry

D W

S

Garage 21-4x19-4

Din

R

Dn

Great Rm. 23-5x24-4

Br 2 15-10x11-9

Covered Porch

Entry

L

MBr 12-4x15-4

L

vaulted

**To order this plan, visit the Menards Building Materials Desk.**

*Berrybridge*

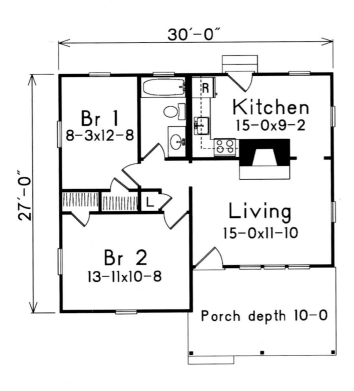

30'-0"

27'-0"

Br 1
8-3x12-8

Kitchen
15-0x9-2

R

L

Living
15-0x11-10

Br 2
13-11x10-8

Porch depth 10-0

## Covered Porch Adds To Perfect Outdoor Getaway

733 total square feet of living area

### Special features

- Bedrooms are separate from the kitchen and living area for privacy
- Lots of closet space throughout this home
- Centrally located bath is easily accessible
- Kitchen features a door accessing the outdoors and a door separating it from the rest of the home
- 2 bedrooms, 1 bath
- Pier foundation

### Price Code AAA

## Springwood

## Country Charm Wrapped In A Veranda

2,059 total square feet of living area

### Special features

- Octagon-shaped breakfast room offers plenty of windows and creates a view to the veranda
- First floor master bedroom has a large walk-in closet and deluxe bath
- 9' ceilings throughout the home
- Secondary bedrooms and bath feature dormers and are adjacent to the cozy sitting area
- 3 bedrooms, 2 1/2 baths, 2-car detached garage
- Slab foundation, drawings also include basement and crawl space foundations

### Price Code C

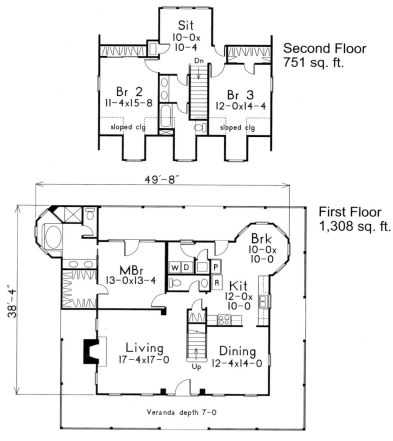

Second Floor 751 sq. ft.

First Floor 1,308 sq. ft.

**To order this plan, visit the Menards Building Materials Desk.**

*Rockspring*

## Style And Economics Meet

1,839 total square feet of living area

### Special features

- Energy efficient home with 2" x 6" exterior walls
- An abundance of front-facing windows helps to keep this berm home bright and cheerful
- The centrally located kitchen easily serves the more formal living and dining rooms as well as the casual family room
- The master bedroom enjoys private access to the bath
- 3 bedrooms, 1 bath
- Slab foundation

### Price Code C

*Thornton*

## Efficient Ranch For A Slender Lot

**1,171 total square feet of living area**

### Special features

- This home is perfect for a starter home, second home on a lake or countryside setting
- The vaulted living room offers many exciting features including a corner fireplace and dining area with sliding doors to the side patio
- A built-in pantry, vaulted ceiling and breakfast bar are just a few amenities of the delightful kitchen
- 3 bedrooms, 2 baths, 2-car garage
- Basement foundation, drawings also include slab and crawl space foundations

### Price Code AA

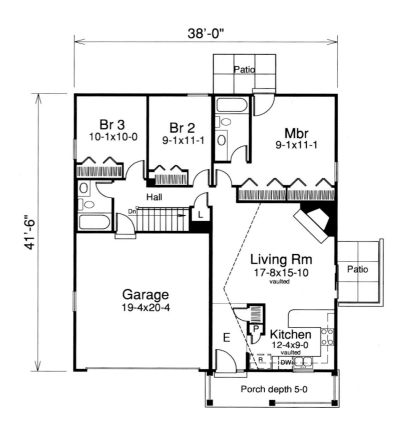

**To order this plan, visit the Menards Building Materials Desk.**

*Woodridge*

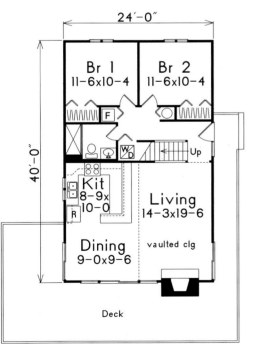

24'-0"

40'-0"

Br 1
11-6x10-4

Br 2
11-6x10-4

F

W
D

Up

Kit
8-9x
10-0

R

Living
14-3x19-6

vaulted clg

Dining
9-0x9-6

Deck

First Floor
960 sq. ft.

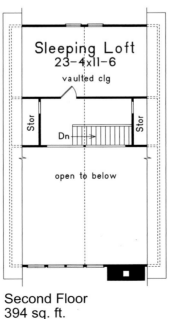

Sleeping Loft
23-4x11-6

vaulted clg

Stor

Dn

Stor

open to below

Second Floor
394 sq. ft.

## Leisure Living With Interior Surprise

1,354 total square feet of living area

### Special features

- Soaring ceilings highlight the kitchen, living and dining areas creating dramatic excitement
- A spectacular large deck surrounds the front and both sides of the home
- An impressive U-shaped kitchen has a wrap-around breakfast bar and shares fantastic views with both the first and second floors through an awesome wall of glass
- Two bedrooms with a bath, a sleeping loft and second floor balcony overlooking the living area complete the home
- 2 bedrooms, 1 bath
- Crawl space foundation

**Price Code A**

# Home Plan Index